SONGLINES IN MICHAELTREE

SONGLINES IN MICHAELTREE

New and Collected Poems

▶▶

Michael S. Harper

University of Illinois Press   Urbana and Chicago

Library of Congress Cataloging-in-Publication Data
Harper, Michael S., 1938–
Songlines in Michaeltree : new and collected poems / Michael S. Harper.
p.   cm.
Includes index.
ISBN 0-252-02144-4 (alk. paper)
I. Title.
PS3558.A6248S64   2000
811'.54—dc21   99-050496

C 5 4 3 2 1

Psalm

Strange
that a harp
of a thousand
strings
should stay
in tune
so long

for Katherine Johnson Harper
1913–88
in memoriam

Acknowledgments

Thanks to the Corporation of Yaddo (YADDO, over and over).

Some of the poems in this book were taken from *History Is Your Own Heartbeat* (1971), *Nightmare Begins Responsibility* (1975), *Healing Song for the Inner Ear* (1985), *Images of Kin* (1977), and *Honorable Amendments* (1995), which were published by the University of Illinois Press.

The poems from *Debridement* were published in 1973 by Doubleday and Co., Inc.

Some poems were taken from *Dear John, Dear Coltrane* (1970) and *Song: I Want a Witness* (1972), which were originally published by the University of Pittsburgh Press.

"My Mother's Bible" and "Shaharazad" first appeared in *The Family Sequences,* which was published as a limited edition in 1998 by Ziggurat Press.

Some poems first appeared in these journals:

African American Review: "An Umbrella of Maple Leaves"; "The Writer's Desk"
American Scholar: "If You Don't Force It"; "The Poet's Voice"; "Release: Kind of Blue"
Bloomsbury Review: "A Coltrane Poem: September 23, 1998"
Callaloo: "Aborigines (Estonia)"; "At the Moment"; "Day Room: St. Elizabeths Hospital"; "Messages as Translation"
Crazy Horse: "Faulkner's Centennial Poem: September 25, 1997"
Field: "Triple Sorbet"
Green Mountain Review: "Achebe at the Bridge"; "Peace Plan: Meditation on the Nine Stages of 'Peacemaking' as a Tribute to Senator *Claiborne Pell:* January 9, 1997"
Luna: "Rhythmic Arrangements (On Prosody)"
Ploughshares: "Irish Suit"; "Strands"
River City: "Advice to Clinton"; "John Hope Franklin"
Shenandoah: "Calligraphy"
TriQuarterly: "The Love Letters of Helen Pitts Douglass"; "Matchbook: The Spinnaker (Sausalito)"; "Patrice Lumumba"

"How to Forgive the Father Who Screams at His Son" and "Paradise (Gihon River, Johnson, Vermont)" were first published in *The New Bread Loaf Anthology of*

Contemporary American Poetry, ed. Michael Collier and Stanley Plumly (London: Hanover, 1999).

"Notes on Making: The Heroic Pattern Updated: 1997" was first published in *Monologue 2,* the catalog for an art exhibition at Cornell University, 1997.

"Reading from Isherwood's Letter Circa 1959–63" first appeared in *The Isherwood Century: Essays on the Life and Work of Christopher Isherwood,* ed. James J. Berg and Chris Freeman (Madison: University of Wisconsin Press, 2000).

"Double Sorbet," "Sorbet," and "Wizardry: The Poetic Saga in Song of Gwendolyn Brooks" first appeared in *The Furious Flowering of African American Poetry,* ed. Joanne V. Gabbin (Charlottesville: University of Virginia Press, 1999).

Special thanks to Deborah Murphy, Graeme Fordyce, and Lisa Giaffo for assisting the poet in articulating his vision, with manuscripts, photographic psychographs, archival retrievals, note preparation, and electronic vigilance to oversights and elisions.

Contents

Poems from

    Dear John, Dear Coltrane (1970)   1

    History Is Your Own Heartbeat (1971)   31

    Song: I Want a Witness (1972)   55

    Debridement (1973)   83

    Nightmare Begins Responsibility (1975)   99

    Images of Kin (1977)   121

    Healing Song for the Inner Ear (1985)   141

    Honorable Amendments (1995)   193

Peace Gene   223

If You Don't Force It   323

To the Reader   369

Notes on Form and Fictions   371

Notes to the Poems   375

Index of Titles   387

When there is no history
When there is no history
When there is no history

there is no metaphor;
there is no metaphor;
there is no metaphor;

a blind nation in storm
a blind nation in storm
a blind nation in storm

mauls its own harbors:
mauls its own harbors:
mauls its own harbors:

sperm whale, Indian, black,
sperm whale, Indian, black,
sperm whale, Indian, black,

belted in these ruins.
belted in these ruins.
belted in these ruins.

From *Dear John, Dear Coltrane*
1970

A friend told me
He'd risen above jazz.
I leave him there.

Brother John

Black man:
I'm a black man;
I'm black; I am—
A black man; black—
I'm a black man;
I'm a black man;
I'm a man; black—
I am—

Bird, buttermilk, bird—
smack, booze and bitches
I am Bird
baddest nightdreamer
on sax in the ornithology-world
I can fly—higher, high, higher—
I'm a black man;
I am; I'm a black man—

Miles, blue haze,
Miles high, another bird,
more Miles, mute,
Mute Miles, clean,
bug-eyed, unspeakable,
Miles, sweet Mute,
sweat Miles, black Miles;
I'm a black man;
I'm black; I am;
I'm a black man—

Trane, Coltrane; John Coltrane;
it's tranetime; chase the Trane;
it's a slow dance;
it's the Trane
in Alabama; acknowledgment,
a love supreme,
it's black Trane; black;
I'm a black man; I'm black;
I am; I'm a black man—

Brother John, Brother John
plays no instrument;
he's a black man; black;
he's a black man; he is
Brother John; Brother John—

I'm a black man; I am;
black; I am; I'm a black
man; I am; I am;
I'm a black man;
I'm a black man;
I am; I'm a black man;
I am:

Alone

A friend told me
He'd risen above jazz.
I leave him there.

Village Blues

(After a Story by John O. Stewart)

The birds flit
in the blue palms,
the cane workers wait,
the man hangs
twenty feet above;
he must come down;
they wait for the priest.
The flies ride on the carcass
which sways like cork in a circle.
The easter light pulls him west.
The priest comes, a man
sunken with rum,
his face sandpapered
into a rouge of split
and broken capillaries.
His duty is the cutting
down of this fruit
of this quiet village
and he staggers slowly, coming.

Elvin's Blues

Sniffed, dilating my nostrils,
the cocaine creeps up my
leg, smacks into my groin;
naked with a bone for luck,
I linger in stickiness,
tickled in the joints;
I will always be high—

Tired of fresh air,
the stone ground bread,
the humid chant of music
which has led me here,
I reed my song:

"They called me the black
narcissus as I devoured
'the white hopes'
crippled in their inarticulate
madness,
Crippled myself,
Drums, each like porcelain
chamber pots, upside down,
I hear a faggot insult my
white wife with a sexless grin,
maggots under his eyelids,
a candle of my fistprint
breaks the membrane of his nose.
Now he stutters."

Last Thursday, I lay with you
tincturing your womb
with aimless strokes I could not feel.
Swollen and hard the weekend,
penitent, inane
I sank into your folds,
or salved your pastel tits,
but could not come.

Sexless as a pimp
dying in performance
like a flare gone down,
the tooth of your pier
hones near the wharf.
The ocean is breathing,
its cautious insomnia—
driven here and there—
with only itself to love.

For Bud

Could it be, Bud
that in slow galvanized
fingers beauty seeped
into *bop* like Bird
weed and Diz clowned—
Sugar waltzing
back into dynamite,
sweetest left hook you
ever dug, baby;
could it violate violence
Bud, like Leadbelly's
chaingang chuckle,
the candied yam
twelve string clutch
of all blues:
there's no rain
anywhere, soft
enough for you.

Discovery

We lay together, darkness all around,
I listen to her constant breath,
and when I thought she slept,
I too fell asleep.
But something stirred me, why I . . .
she was staring at me with her eyes,
her breasts still sturdy,
her thigh warming mine.
And I, a little shaken as she stroked
my skin and kissed my brow,
reached for the light turned on,
feeling for the heat which would
reveal how long she had looked
and cared.
The bulb was hot.   It burned my hand.

The Black Angel

Childhood games,
played without innocence,
and in place of the angel,
take me to a grove of pepper trees;
they lighten my head.
Trees emit their odors,
a natural oxygen tent;
have you noticed the air is heavy
in trees that shed their leaves
without hesitance,
and flow with sap,
and are closest
to the angel's skin;
the eyes, each singly
wide, smarting, unreadable
as the sap, and which
recount the games,
verses, puzzles of other men:
I am reading poems
to this black angel.
Kindled in the shrill
eloquence of other men,
the angel forces open my hands
and in the palms
leaves her footprints.

Clark's Way West: Another Version

The venereal moon
draws six women
to the Missouri River
where they empty their
beaver pelt children
in great Montana falls
near Indian prairie slope.
From the rattler's rattle
their labor was eased
and the children came
from their collective blindness
to the Shawnee burial ground:
each child is blind.
The earth is not invalid here,
the grizzly slaps at salmon,
and stops, and retreats;
and the children bob
down the falls to the basin below.

Remember Mexico

Villages of high quality
merchandise—hand tooled leather,
blown glass like diamonds,
cloth finer than linen,
delicious food without dysentery,
mountain water from palapa groves
cured by glistening rocks,
burro-drawn carts for the day,
fishing boats destined for clear
water and giant marlin;
the peasants clean
tanned and bilingual;
lemon, papaya,
horseback or raft,
turtle in the picnic
baskets, white lunch
on hacienda siesta—
pure and unblemished
in the public notices.

I remember the birds
of the desert
ripping a horse
not yet fallen;
hookworm, beetles,
the soup of the desert;
cows and donkeys
eat around the cracked
and broken American
automobiles; in this covey
of linkage, spoken here,
I think of Montezuma's

unspeakable rites
in honed rock graves—
bloodmeal and black tunnels;
Indians who speak no Spanish
and worship the sea,
fruit unpicked in suspect
sweetness for corn,
diesel smoke forcing
Indian, and Indian
and Indian, and Indian
farther up the mountainside.

Zocalo

We stand pinned
to the electric mural
of Mexican history
and listen to a paid guide
explain fresco technique
and the vision of Diego Rivera:
Cortés, crippled with disease,
his Indian woman and son,
sailor raping an Indian
in frocks of priesthood.

In the center the Mexican
eagle peels the serpent
and cools his thirst on desert cactus;
Hidalgo forced into Independence,
that bald creole iconoclast
lost east of Guadalajara;
near him, Montezuma
passively meets Cortés,
salutes the Gods,
dies, the mistake of his people;
corn mixes with chickens and goats,
housepets, muskets and cactus wine.

To your left Rockefeller,
Morgan, the atomic bomb,
Wall Street, the pipeline to the Vatican;
below, the Mexican people pay
for the chosen friar
and the dignity of retreat
to the hills above the central valley.

Then comes Juarez—our guide's
voice rings with full-blooded pride
at the full-blooded Indian
busting the military;
he disbands the church,
opens his arms, and gives
the land to the people.
Our guide is speaking in Spanish:
"You see, my friends, we want the land
that Santa Anna gave you for ten
million pesos; we want Texas, Arizona
and the rest of the west;
take the painting, absorb it—
then give us back our land."

Black Spring

We gave it life, mahogany hands,
loose in song;
we gave it to children
in paraffin—
our biology.
It grew lovely and indecent
into a female orchid,
and, of course, produced
children of its own.
We took it back again.

Blues Alabama

She's blacker
than the night which holds
us in our communion
against the white picket fences.
There's clash in her eyes,
and she smiles whitely
to the tambourines.
There's a folk song audience
of rebels who lover
her mother into children,
and then the children,
and they're all in the roads
searching for the art
which makes singing
a blessing of hatred.

American History

Those four black girls blown up
in that Alabama church
remind me of five hundred
middle passage blacks,
in a net, under water
in Charleston harbor
so *redcoats* wouldn't find them.
Can't find what you can't see
can you?

We Assume: On the Death of Our Son, Reuben Masai Harper

We assume
that in twenty-eight hours,
lived in a collapsible isolette,
you learned to accept pure oxygen
as the natural sky;
the scant shallow breaths
that filled those hours
cannot, did not make you fly—
but dreams were there
like crooked palmprints on
the twin-thick windows of the nursery—
in the glands of your mother.

We assume
the sterile hands
drank chemicals in and out
from lungs opaque with mucus,
pumped your stomach,
eeked the bicarbonate in
crooked, green-winged veins,
out in a plastic mask;

A woman who'd lost her first son
consoled us with an angel gone ahead
to pray for our family—
gone into that sky
seeking oxygen,
gone into autopsy,
a fine brown powdered sugar,
a disposable cremation:

We assume
you did not know we loved you.

Reuben, Reuben

I reach from pain
to music great enough
to bring me back,
swollenhead, madness,
lovefruit, a pickle of hate
so sour my mouth twicked
up and would not sing;
there's nothing in the beat
to hold it in
melody and turn human skin;
a brown berry gone
to rot just two days on the branch;
we've lost a son,
the music, *jazz,* comes in.

Deathwatch

Twitching in the cactus
hospital gown, a loon
on hairpin wings,
she tells me how
her episiotomy
is perfectly sewn
and doesn't hurt
while she sits in a pile
of blood
which once cleaned
the placenta
my third son should be in.
She tells me how early
he is, and how strong,
like his father,
and long, like a black-
stemmed Easter rose
in a white hand.

Just under five pounds
you lie there, a collapsed
balloon doll, burst in your
fifteenth hour, with the face
of your black father,
his fingers, his toes,
and eight voodoo
adrenalin holes in
your pinwheeled hair-lined
chest; you witness
your parents sign the autopsy
and disposal papers

shrunken to duplicate
in black ink
on white paper
like the country
you were born in,
unreal, asleep,
silent, almost alive.

This is a dedication
to our memory
of three sons—
two dead, one alive—
a reminder of a letter
to Du Bois
from a student
at Cornell—on behalf
of his whole history class.
The class is confronted
with a question,
and no one—
not even the professor—
is sure of the answer:
"Will you please tell us
whether or not it is true
that negroes
are not able to cry?"

America needs a killing.
America needs a killing.
Survivors will be human.

Molasses and the Three Witches

Inside out, the police announce
there's a riot—on CBS—
it's a barnfire.
Firemen and police
Ball-eye into the squares:
this is the first barnfire
in history.
Roll 'em:
Lady says she saw
the first keg of molasses
in a gunny sack
on a huge black's back;
a black rosebush
on his big-eared helper;
flour and grits
in a pelt as soft as snow—
all gone up in the smoke
of the last spiritual
of Br'ers Bear,
Rabbit, Fox—
the black trinity:
I will not go quietly—
I will not go quietly—
I will not go quietly—

Dear John, Dear Coltrane

a love supreme, a love supreme
a love supreme, a love supreme

Sex fingers toes
in the marketplace
near your father's church
in Hamlet, North Carolina—
witness to this love
in this calm fallow
of these minds,
there is no substitute for pain:
genitals gone or going,
seed burned out,
you tuck the roots in the earth,
turn back, and move
by river through the swamps,
singing: *a love supreme, a love supreme;*
what does it all mean?
Loss, so great each black
woman expects your failure
in mute change, the seed gone.
You plod up into the electric city—
your song now crystal and
the blues. You pick up the horn
with some will and blow
into the freezing night:
a love supreme, a love supreme—

Dawn comes and you cook
up the thick sin 'tween
impotence and death, fuel

the tenor sax cannibal
heart, genitals, and sweat
that makes you clean—
a love supreme, a love supreme—

Why you so black?
cause I am
why you so funky?
cause I am
why you so black?
cause I am
why you so sweet?
cause I am
why you so black?
cause I am
a love supreme, a love supreme:

So sick
you couldn't play *Naima,*
so flat we ached
for song you'd concealed
with your own blood,
your diseased liver gave
out its purity,
the inflated heart
pumps out, the tenor kiss,
tenor love:
a love supreme, a love supreme—
a love supreme, a love supreme—

A Mother Speaks:
The Algiers Motel Incident, Detroit

It's too dark to see black
in the windows of Woodward
or Virginia Park.
The undertaker
pushed his body back
into place
with plastic and gum
but it wouldn't
hold water.
When I looked
for marks
or lineament
or fine stitching
I was led away
without seeing
this plastic
face they'd built
that was not my son's.
They tied the eye
torn out
by shotgun
into place
and his shattered
arm cut away
with his buttocks
that remained.
My son's gone
by white hands
though he said
to his last word—
"Oh I'm so sorry,
officer, I broke your gun."

Mr. P.C.

Paul Laurence Dunbar Chambers—
what a long history
of perfection, bass man,
those swollen solos
on Miles's Standard
teachings—"Blues"
    G

      D

        A

            G

        D

If Mingus is monster
star, you are his
private brother, so soft
baby, so beauteous
in your shuffling,
how many soundful
dysplexia did you do it
over and over and over
do it to everybody's gutstrings
listening as flat out,
Jim, as harpheart and bone—
What a long history
Paul Laurence Dunbar Chambers,
and your namesakes,
in the chambers.

Biafra Blues

Another brother gone
another brother gone
another brother gone
another brother gone
another brother gone
another brother gone

Gray hair and puffed bellies
the stomach moves out
to its specialty—
floating children first,
without smiles
The Soviet Union
lays it out
on the consumers
starving
on the oil slick
whites of their eyes;
the Red Cross
bandages
the refugee
camps in a white
blockade:

another brother gone
another brother gone
another brother gone
another brother gone
another brother gone
another brother gone

Egyptian pilots
cash the American checks—
Lagos, old England,
Washington
are animal kingdoms
in the guts of war:
there is no war
that's not famine
members of the UN

Biafra is an eastern
community in revolt
across territorial lines
worked out with a European
compass: fathom the sectioning
off Biafra—

There is no famine
there is no genocide
only a community
in revolt, only
the refinement of oil
slicks, only a black
smell, sunken, aglow:

another brother gone
another brother gone
another brother gone
another brother gone
another brother gone
another brother gone

From *History Is Your Own Heartbeat*
1971

For this reason Martin is dead;
for this reason Malcolm is dead;
for this reason Coltrane is dead;
in the eyes of my first son are the browns
of these men and their music.

Prayer: Mt. Hood and Environs

The windows of America
are faceless, incestuous screens
pumiced in pure glass,
triangular, innocent,
wired white hoods
cropped in green grass.

Comatose and armed
explorers brought salt water
from the ocean to boil
in three kettles as an offering;

The Indians smoked
on the mountaintrails
in buck heat
high along the Columbia;

Lewis and Clark,
their slave, York,
took their salt up
in their webbings;

the meat now cured,
the lumber stink off
the river,
fertilize no soil
without Indian blood
or red roses.

Love Medley: Patrice Cuchulain

"Stirrups, leggings, a stainless
steel slide, a dishpan, sheet,
a thread spool, scissors,
three facemasks, smocks, paper
overshoes, a two-way mirror, dials:"
the head and left arm
cruise out, almost together,
and you drop into gloves,
your own ointment
pulling your legs
binding your cord; the cheesed
surface skin, your dark
hairless complexion, the metallic room,
orchestrate and blow up your lungs,
clogged on protein and vitamins,
for the sterile whine of the delivery
room and your staff of attendants.
It is free exercise when the cord's
cut; you weigh in for the clean up
as your mother gets her local
for her stitches: boy, 6' 13".

As you breathe easily, your mother's
mother is tubed and strapped,
hemorrhaging slowly from her varices;
your two dead brothers who could
not breathe are berries
gone to rot at our table:
what is birth but death
with complexity: blood, veins,
machinery and love: our names.

This Is My Son's Song: *"Ungie, Hi Ungie"*

A two-year-old boy
is a blossom in the intensive
care aisle, small as
a ball-bearing,
round, open, and smooth;
for a month, in his first
premature hours, his shaved
head made him a mohawk Indian
child, tubes the herbs
for his nest, a collapsed lung
the bulbous wing of a hawk.
Slivered into each sole
is an intravenous solution
to balance his losses
or what they take out
for the lab; the blue spot
on his spine is a birth
mark of needle readings;
the hardened thighs immune
from 70 shots of various
drugs of uneven depth; the chest
is thick with congestion: bad
air and mucus—good air and pure
oxygen; jerky pouch buffalo lungs—
It does not surprise me
when he waits patiently for his
grandmother, over her five-hour
painless operation; he has
waited in his isolette
before: the glow in his eyes
is for himself, will and love:
an exclamation of your name:
"Ungie, hi Ungie"; you are saved.

History as Bandages:
Polka Dots and Moonbeams

One is an igloo
of whalebone and oil
and a poisonous gas;
one is a canoe under water
laden with wild rice,
grubs, and Indian arrows;
one is a banjo
packed with thin dirt
in Richmond, Virginia:
Gabriel: 1800;
one is a round bubble
of mustard rock
broken on an Indian squaw;
one is a print of a buffalo,
bearded, masked, made
musty skinned hair.

The white rectangular
patchwork covers all these
national wounds kept
secretly bound, at night,
absorbing color and blood and bones
of all shapes and disguises.

Here Where Coltrane Is

Soul and race
are private dominions,
memories and modal
songs, a tenor blossoming,
which would paint suffering
a clear color, but is not in
this Victorian house
without oil in zero degree
weather and a forty-mile-an-hour wind;
it is all a well-knit family:
a love supreme.
Oak leaves pile up on walkway
and steps, catholic as apples
in a special mist of clear white
children who love my children.
I play "Alabama"
on a warped record player
skipping the scratches
on your faces over the fibrous
conical hairs of plastic
under the wooden floors.

Dreaming on a train from New York
to Philly, you hand out six
notes which become an anthem
to our memories of you:
oak, birch, maple,
apple, cocoa, rubber.
For this reason Martin is dead;
for this reason Malcolm is dead;
for this reason Coltrane is dead;
in the eyes of my first son are the browns
of these men and their music.

Martin's Blues

He came apart in the open,
the slow motion cameras
falling quickly
neither alive nor kicking;
stone blind dead
on the balcony
that old melody
etched his black lips
in a pruned echo:
We shall overcome
some day—
Yes we did!
Yes we did!

Madimba: Gwendolyn Brooks

Music is its own heartbeat

Double-conscious sister in the veil,
Double-conscious sister in the veil;
Double-conscious sister in the veil:
Double-conscious sister in the veil.

You beat out the pulse with your mallets,
the brown wishbone anemones
unflowered and unworn in Chicago congo
prints, images, otherness, images

from the fossilbank: Madimba.
Black Man; I'm a black man; black—
A-um-ni-pad-me-hum—
another brother gone:

"the first act of liberation
is to destroy one's cage"—
a love supreme;
a love supreme.

Images: words: language
typing the round forms: Juneteenth,
baby, we free, free at last:
black man, I'm a black man.

A garden is a manmade vision,
rectangular, weeded, shelled,
pathed, hosed, packed in,
covered with manure, pruned;

I own you; you're mine, you
mine, baby: to bear unborn things.
Double-conscious sister in the veil:
Double-conscious sister in the veil.

Black woman: America is artful
outside time, ideal outside space;
you its only machine: Madimba:
Double-conscious sister in the veil.

Photographs: A Vision of Massacre

We thought the grass
would grow up quickly
to hide the bodies.
A brother sloped across
his brother, the patched
clay road slipping
into our rainy season
of red, our favorite color.

When the pictures came
we spoke of our love
for guns, oiled and glistening
in the rich blood of machines:
bodies, boys and girls, clutching
their private parts, oiled,
now slightly pink,
and never to be used.

The Dance of the Elephants

PART 1

The trains ran through the eleven
nights it took to vacate the town;
relatives and lovers tacked in a row
on the button-board sidings,
wails of children tossed in a pile
wails of women tossed in a salad
to be eaten with soap and a rinse.
Those who took all they had to the borders,
those who took their bottles
three centuries old, those who
thought only of language, the written
word, are forgiven.
One daughter is riding on the train
above her mother, above her mother,
into the tunnel of the elephants.

Culture tells us most about its animals
singing our children asleep, or let them
slip into a room as smoothly as
refrigeration.

PART 2

To be comforted by Swiss music
is a toy elephant in a box,
skimming the nickelplated air.
Beethoven's a passion dance
forgotten in a stamped coin—
it is magic—it is magic—

We dance the old beast 'round the fireplace,
coal engines fuming in a row,
elephant chimes in a toy rain—
human breath skimming the air.

We skim the air—
it is magic—the engines
smelling the chimes,
Beethoven chiming the magic—
we escape it on a train.

Sung in America,
the song some telescopic sight,
a nickelplated cream,
a small girl cuddles her elephant,
the song in the streets
leaping the train windows,
and what love as the elephant chimes.

from an anecdote
by Susan Kirschner

House on Miramar, San Francisco

Five years in the house
of pisces, the bellbottom
faces of sons
all shining the mantel mirror
and the fireplace
stacked with matches,
weeds, the dead books
curled to unworkable precision;
the western sun bleeds
through the seasonal fog,
the belly of woman
pregnant and puffy
with seeds from African pottery
or the song of Billie Holiday
on a big band of air.

Breeze from the open fireplace,
the wind crookeyes down the flue,
black ashes of newsprint and cartons
milky and burnt: incineration.
What they did to no. 2 and 3 sons:
firebombed from the Kaiser nursery,
the phlegm and algae cut away:
medicinal incineration;
what they did to this young girl
in the late cot sun
is the workbench history of disease.

Dahlias in the yard
the bulbs hammering up
as snails after milky submersion;
flower and weed,
crossbreeded boys sway
on the rusty trapeze
of their mother's hipbones
bent and billowy,
womanous nursery with dugs.

Cherokee skin, Indian
colors, bushes, sanitary
padding, ridges of woman
broken and panting in the sun.

Movin' Wes

Gone from us
this guitar
where the bull resides
his heat
gone from us,
Movin' Wes rides
his beginnings:

Wes, guitar, Movin' Wes:
Charlie Christian
Movin' Wes
Leadbelly, Movin' Wes
John Lee Hooker
Movin' Wes
B. B. King, Movin' Wes
Wes Montgomery,
Movin' Wes:

Shaped like a heart
this guitar is its own organ;
its gnarled hands
bled octaves
in men's veins,
their children
the stickpin controls:
Movin' Wes:

Gone from us,
electronic ears
tune on
Movin' Wes:

Unrecorded,
Movin' Wes
blew with Trane
"Favorite Things"
so hard, out there,
guitar became man:
Movin' Wes:

Instrument
Favorite Things
all alive:
Movin' Wes:

Newsletter from My Mother:
8:30 A.M., December 8, '69

"1100 Exposition
4115 South Central
and some place on 55th Street
were all subject to siege
at 5:30 this morning.
The police arrived with search warrants.

"At the present time
1100 Exposition
and the house on 55th Street
have fallen.

"4115 South Central
is still resisting;
they have sandbagged
the place and are wearing
bullet-proof vests,
tear gas masks;

"the whole area is cordonned off,
Wadsworth School is closed;
the police are clearing a hotel
next door to get a better vantage.

"The police deny this is part
of a nationwide program to wipe
out the Panther Party;
one of the fellows here at work,
who lives in the area,
says that they were clearing the streets
last night, arresting people
on any pretext,
and that the jails are full.

"(I have to wait until my boss
starts her class in the conference
room so I can turn on the radio
and get the latest news.)

"10 A.M.:
The Panthers are surrendering
1 at a time."

"*Bird Lives*": Charles Parker in St. Louis

Last on legs, last on sax,
last in Indian wars, last on *smack,*
Bird is specious, *Bird* is alive,
horn, unplayable, before, after,
right now: it's heroin time:
smack, in the melody a trip;
smack, in the Mississippi;
smack, in the drug merchant trap;
smack, in St. Louis, Missouri.

We knew you were through—
trying to get out of town,
unpaid bills, connections
unmet, unwanted, unasked,
Bird's in the last arc
of his own light: *blow Bird!*
And you did—
screaming, screaming, baby,
for life, after it, around it,
screaming for life, *blow Bird!*

What is the meaning of music?
What is the meaning of war?
What is the meaning of oppression?
Blow Bird! Ripped up and down
into the interior of life, the pain,
Bird, the embraceable you,
how many brothers gone,
smacked out: blues and racism,
the hardest, longest penis
in the Mississippi urinal:
Blow Bird!

Taught more musicians, then forgot,
space loose, fouling the melodies,
the marching songs, the fine white
geese from the plantations,
syrup in this pork barrel,
Kansas City, the even teeth
of the mafia, the big band:
Blow Bird! Inside out Charlie's
guts, *Blow Bird!* get yourself killed.

In the first wave, the musicians,
out there, alone, in the first wave;
everywhere you went, Massey Hall,
Sweden, New Rochelle, *Birdland,*
nameless bird, Blue Note, Carnegie,
tuxedo junction, out of nowhere,
confirmation, confirmation, confirmation:
Bird Lives! Bird Lives! and you do:
Dead—

High Modes: Vision as Ritual: Confirmation

Black Man Go Back To The Old Country
Black Man Go Back To The Old Country
Black Man Go Back To The Old Country
Black Man Go Back To The Old Country

And you went back home for the images,
the brushwork packing the mud
into the human form; and the ritual:
Black Man Go Back To The Old Country.

We danced, the chocolate trees and samba
leaves wetting the paintbrush, and babies
came in whispering of one, oneness,
otherness, forming each man in his music,
one to one: and we touched, *contact-high,*
high modes, *contact-high,* and the images,
contact-high, man to man, came back.
Black Man Go Back To The Old Country.

The grooves turned in a human face,
Lady Day, blue and green, modally,
and we touched, *contact-high,* high modes:
Black Man Go Back To The Old Country.

Bird was a mode from the old country;
Bud Powell bowed in modality, blow Bud;
Louis Armstrong touched the old country,
and brought it back, around corners;
Miles is a mode; Coltrane is, power,
Black Man Go Back To The Old Country
Black Man Go Back To The Old Country
Black Man Go Back To The Old Country

And we go back to the well: Africa,
the first mode, and man, modally,
touched the land of the continent,
modality: we are one; a man is another
man's face, modality, in continuum,
from man, to man, *contact-high,* to man,
contact-high, to man, high modes, oneness,
contact-high, man to man, *contact-high:*

Black Man Go Back To The Old Country
Black Man Go Back To The Old Country
Black Man Go Back To The Old Country
Black Man Go Back To The Old Country

From *Song: I Want a Witness*
1972

Three things hinder . . . : to see the good to be done
and to neglect it; to hesitate when the occasion
presents itself; to know evil and follow it.

Song: *I Want a Witness*

Blacks in frame houses
call to the helicopters,
their antlered arms
spinning; jeeps pad
these glass-studded streets;
on this hill are tanks painted gold.

Our children sing
spirituals of *Motown,*
idioms these streets suckled
on a southern road.
This scene is about power,
terror, producing
love and pain and pathology;
in an army of white dust,
blacks here to *testify*
and *testify,* and *testify,*
and *redeem,* and *redeem,*
in black smoke coming,
as they wave their arms,
as they wave their tongues.

Kneading

She kneads the kernels, grains,
powder of the filled containers,
and makes the bread that fuses
my sons and the world of the house,
and the dust is a resin of her face,
and she is kneading again.

With a scar shaped like an anchor,
an inch-long break at the wrist
where she hammered the window jamb,
and the soft belly of my own furred
animals, these sons quiver in the shadows
of her dress, faced into the crevices
of her tenderness, and the kneading.

The two absent boys who linger in the bread
of the kneading hands, in the eyes
and ears of the mother, kneading,
go, back and forth, with their real
brothers, hitching themselves to these germs;
and their father chews the meat
that passes into their mouths,
these juices from kneading, these gums
torn with the teeth of death, the death
of those like them, living, and eating
this kneaded bread, their mother's
and their father's kneading, this meat.

Dead Oaks

I eat on all fours
over the dank hole
where my two-hundred-year-
old oak once was
now in a pile at
the cord-wound corral.
I think of the smell
of this earth,
earth that poisons
this brimmed cemetery,
burial ground
long since forgotten.

On a farm in the eastern
half of this state,
an old woman sat
on her porch whistling
an Indian tune
through whittling
in Norwegian.

I listen to her son
sing of the death of his
brother in war,
his brothers dying
in the old ancestral
earth of the Far East
or in African mines
plaqued in its gold
to our commercial hearth.

I chop at the tree
to make kindling
as the fire arches
out of sight, food
in this old place, this hole
in the cosmic earth.

Pale in this death heat,
the son of the mother
on the porch, having
heard of her death,
reading of his brother's
death, reading of the death
of his brothers:
Indian, Norwegian,
sits on this old stump
and whittles, whistling:
congress of the last
poetic word, this damp
ceremonial hill, this oak.

Oak

She lifts the two boys on
the overturned rowboat, a galley
plank as a slide;
gummy paint on the underside
sticks to their shoes;
as they walk the eggshell
white blackens the swaying birch boat.

She lifts cracked plaster,
glass, rock from the foundation,
hunting for nails, her pigtailed
sway the break of oars
beating the lake overturned;
she works for new grass
that springs up, the three oaks
burned to death in winter,
mistook victims of our rubbish pile.
A hundred-gallon garbage can
freezes in its burned tracks;
a wire cylinder holds our burned
paper; near the chain fence
we chew the burned oak
with a two-man saw.

In the attic is an old bed;
I hear its thumping as I watch her
leafing seeds to the hoed land
in foot-deep holes in our thawing ground,
trees that must grow in gravel.

We begin to live in the old way:
fertile eggs in a poaching tin,
cooked meal, kneaded bread rising
on the open-air rack,
stumps at our garden table.

As the spring thaws she plants,
uncovers, hoes, digs for the rich
earth; in gravel we take up the saw;
in the old way we cut dead oak.

Last Affair: Bessie's Blues Song

Disarticulated
arm torn out,
large veins cross
her shoulder intact,
her tourniquet
her blood in all-white big bands:

Can't you see
what love and heartache's done to me
I'm not the same as I used to be
this is my last affair

Mail truck or parked car
in the fast lane,
afloat at forty-three
on a Mississippi road,
Two-hundred-pound muscle on her ham bone,
'nother nigger dead 'fore noon.

Can't you see
what love and heartache's done to me
I'm not the same as I used to be
this is my last affair

Fifty-dollar record
cut the vein in her neck,
fool about her money
toll her black train wreck,
white press missed her fun'ral
in the same stacked deck:

Can't you see
what love and heartache's done to me
I'm not the same as I used to be
this is my last affair

Loved a little blackbird
heard she could sing,
Martha in her vineyard
pestle in her spring,
Bessie had a bad mouth
made my chimes ring:

Can't you see
what love and heartache's done to me
I'm not the same as I used to be
this is my last affair

Homage to the New World

Surrounded by scientists in a faculty
house, the trees wet with hot rain,
grass thickening under the trees,
welcomers come, ones and twos,
gifts of shoehorns, soap, combs,
half a subscription to the courier,
some news about changing
plates, the nearest market,
how to pick up the trash, a gallon
of milk twice a week, OK?

On the third day here,
a friend came in the night to announce
a phone call and a message,
and heard the shell go in
and the rifle cocking,
our next-door animal-vet neighbor,
and cried out, "Don't shoot,"
and walked away to remember the phone
and the message, the crickets,
and the rifle cocking,
grass and hot rain.

I write in the night air
of the music of Coltrane,
the disc of his voice in this
contralto heart, my wife;
so what! Kind of Blue,
these fatherless whites
come to consciousness
with a history of the gun—
the New World, if misery had
a voice, would be a rifle cocking.

PHOTOGRAPHS: *NEGATIVES*

Nightmare begins responsibility.

The Indian is the root of an apple tree;
history, symbol, presence: these voices
are not lost on us, or them.

THE NEGATIVES

She agitates
the quart developing tank
in total darkness,
our windowless bath;
the cylinder slides
inside against the film
for ten minutes
at 70 degrees.
I can see the developer
acid in the luminous
dial of my watch:
she adds the stop-bath.
The hypo fix
fastens the images
hardening against light
on her film and papers.
I imagine her movement
at night as her teeth grind:
I know she dreams of the negatives.

PHOTOGRAPHS

Felt negatives work the pores
coal black in darkness
double negatives;
now in the light
the emulsive side down
on top of brown-gray paper
human images rise.

From bath to workbench
in our tarpaper shack;
stacks of grade paper appear,
fixed images on archival prints;
tempered, the controlled chemicals
edge 'round the contact sheet
edged in a family grave.

Print and stir dektol
on agfa brovira bromide paper,
apply stop action, keep moving
saline amniotic fluid,
dilute with hot water.

The iron water cools;
paper shown to light
turns black
as skin on my arm.

THE NIGHT OF FROST

I walk out in the first
autumn frost over dog
dung, puddin' rock, acorns,
gutted pumpkin, to the last
three letters on the mailbox
at the road; I paste my decals
over the owner's name
as I pull the lid
and stare in.

I walk on the squat rock fence
to our apple tree,
then near the trailer
across the road
where a cyclops woman
with glaucoma
bends in nightclothes
watering her plants.

I walk back over her sold
stone peering at her old house,
the crooked clabbered sidings,
uneven cut window jambs,
slatted tarpaper roof,
cut and hammered into stars.

I walk as negative
image over white crusted
grave stones as my dark feet
stamp their footprints.

AT THE CEMETERY

1

Horton, Smith,
Rose are the landmarks:
Horton the whaler
turned to farming
to sell to the markets,
a nearby street bears
his clan;
the road is Smith,
who rolled two horsedrawn
wagons filled with boulders
from Plymouth Rock;
the weathercock etched
in *Rose* tells directions
on a wooden staff
at the road's edge.

This house is a *Horton*
house, the addition *Rose,*
1830; my sons pedal
in the brimming sand:
Smith, Horton, Rose.

2

They cut to the center,
veer to the apple tree
on this northern border
of the tree line.

A great apple tree
lies on this northern
boundary, its bruised
fruit dropping like flares
among the puddin' stone;
as they climb the tree
their photographs
blacken in their acid
as if burnt by sunlight,
the corners etch and turn up
in their light brimming curls.

Spent birch treelimbs
leave diamond shapes
where the limbs once grew;
they stride in these meters
up the burst limbs,

their feet in diamond
shapes where the limbs were.
I hear the roots underground
turn nosedown
away from bones
toward the artesian line
much much below.

UTILITY ROOM

She shades the prints bathed
in what iron water there is,
artesian iron spring water;
pictures of winter green
blur in darkness,
the second hand stops.

She shakes the developing tank
as a uterus
mixing developer
to the negatives
where no light appears;
I hold her hips
as saline and acid
pock up images.
I see my children
on these negatives
in a windowless room.

A simple enlarger,
a bulb with a shade,
images born through her lens
packed on the contact sheet;
fatted negatives under thick
condenser glass,
prints from her uterus,
cramps from her developing tank.

THE BORNING ROOM

I stand in moonlight
in our borning room,
now a room of closets
changed by the owners.
Once only the old
and newborn slept
on this first floor,
this boarded door
closed now to the hearth
of our wood burning.

I look over the large bed
at the shape of my woman;
there is no image
for her, no place
for the spring child.
Her cornered shape dreams
a green robed daughter
warmed in a bent room
close to fireplace oven,
warmed by an apple tree:
the old tried to make it new,
the new old; we will not die here.

THE FAMILIES ALBUM

Goggled mother with her children
stomp on the tar road,
their dresses black:
sugar maple, white pine,
apple tree, sumac,
young birch, red oak,
pine, cedar, deer moss
watch the archival print
in this death march,
for they lived here,
as they live with us now,
in these slanted pine floors
they tried to straighten,
in these squared windows
unsquared, in wallpaper torn
down, in the bare beams
of the addition plastered,
in a mother's covered eye
diseased by too much light,
too much blood which struck
her husband dead, too much
weed to make the farm work
too many crooked doorways
on a dirt road tarred over.

This old house which was hers
made her crooked back a shingle,
her covered eye this fireplace oven,
her arms the young pine beams
now our clapboard siding;
the covered well runs in this dirt
basement, her spring watering her grave
where the fruit, vegetables, woodpile lie.

TRAYS: A PORTFOLIO

1

At the tray
she looks in the heart
of these negatives,
her borning room
fireplace oven full of pitch,
roasting the brick sidings,
her heart warmed
from the inside cradle
in a windowless bath.

2

Two African veils
on two sons
clothed in their isolettes
burn in a hospital.

3

From a pan of chemicals
the images turn from black
to white flames as we
agitate the quart
tank developer:
black men,
two sons stoppered
from isolette
to incinerator,
a child walks
under her apron
as film develops
in her black and white eyes;
she stoops over the boys
on the primed cut smock,
born, inflated, enlarged.

4

We grade paper from one to six
as our number of children;
little contrast to extreme contrast,
two to four the perfect negative
in our perfect family
enlarged as a light bulb
with a shade; we fight
the dirt on the negatives,
touch up with spotting liquid
absorbed by numbered paper:
contact: print:
blacken our negatives with light.

5

Pumpkin, squash, green
peppers, onions, carrots
squat in cellar piles;
I hear the gargle
of hot water pipes
gushing through copper;
the mice spin between walls
eating paper under my drain;
the waterpump whirs
iron rust in each drain
from artesian fields underground.
From the cellar door
near the boarded well
is a concord grape arbor;
I walk by evergreen seedlings,
verbena bush
looking for cranberries
to harvest as drops of blood
on a weedeaten farm.
In a clot of pines
my sons roll in their bog
in a pool of grass,
each step trundled,
each laugh bedded with blood.

HISTORY AS APPLE TREE

Cocumscussoc is my village,
the western arm of Narragansett
Bay; Canonicus chief sachem;
black men escape into his tribe.

How does patent not breed heresy?
Williams came to my chief
for his tract of land,
hunted by mad Puritans,
founded Providence Plantation;
Seekonk where he lost
first harvest, building, plant,
then the bay from these natives:
he set up trade.
With Winthrop he bought
an island, *Prudence;*
two others, *Hope* and *Patience*
he named, though small.
His trading post at the cove;
Smith's at another close by.
We walk the Pequot trail
as artery or spring.

Wampanoags, Cowesets,
Nipmucks, Niantics
came by canoe for the games;
matted bats, a goal line,
a deerskin filled with moss:
lacrosse. They danced;
we are told they gambled their souls.

In your apple orchard
legend conjures Williams's name;
he was an apple tree.
Buried in his own lot
off Benefit Street
a giant apple tree grew;
two hundred years later,
when the grave was opened,
dust and root grew
in his human skeleton:
bones became apple tree.

As black man I steal away
in the night to the apple tree,
place my arm in the rich grave,
black sachem on a family plot,
take up a chunk of apple root,
let it become my skeleton,
become my own myth:
my arm the historical branch,
my name the bruised fruit,
black human photograph: apple tree.

From *Debridement*
1973

"When a woman take the blues,
she tuck her head and cry.
But when a man catch the blues,
he grab his shoes and slide."

HEARTBLOW

RAT FEVER: HISTORY AS HALLUCINATION

A man's a man
when he can kill
rats with bare hands,
eat them
or be eaten by them.

Tracked leavings
on the village roof,
out the window
sewers overflowing;
a man's a man
when he can eat himself up
and leave no tracks.

NEAR THE WHITE HOUSE

A cross is a machine
in a ship's hull,
an anchor on the Potomac
is a mansion.
This black statue curtseys
in a vanilla smile,
its lips a cross
burning, its heat
flicking the mansion lights:
beacons on the marbleheads
and a sorrow song is a cross.

THE MEANING OF PROTEST

Between the world and me
a black boy is a native
son with a long dream
if a white man will listen.
Uncle Tom's children
were eight men, all outsiders,
fish bellies living
underground.

Pagan Spain taught us the church
was woman as mystery, a penis
the sword to butcher each other;
Black Power! we're not going
to the moon, and in Bandung
white man can't come,
he's on a savage holiday.

Blossoms in a peanut field
won't bring me home;
something in the hum
of cotton is a glue
that won't hold red soil still;
ten million voices spliced
on an iron cross
between the world, and me, and you.

TREE FEVER

Skin of trees cut down,
men in trees,
sacks of scrotum
breastmeat on brims,
soldier hats
on each father patroller,
posse the flag on picnic
their stars and stripes
our skin of scars.

BIGGER'S BLUES

In this case
Mary's mama is correspondent:
blind witch with threaded
needles on the family table.
Ping-pong money to the poor.
Poor Mary gone off C.O.D.
in a golden trunk
head handed to her.
At the furnace where Bigger
hatted up, mama's
touching led him crazy
(what begins with N
and rhymes with Bigger)
on, on, on.

PARABLE

Black-stemmed ax
stuck in white tree;
roots in waterhole
roped underground
get tree fever;
cut off handle,
tree die.

HISTORY AS DIABOLICAL MATERNALISM

When I grind glass
I think of lenses
swallowed like sugar,
a preacher with glass eye,
a eunuch named Jesus,
Black Mary in his cottonfield.

HEARTBLOW: MESSAGES

I sit in cubbyhole,
wasp nests north and south,
woods to the west, ocean east,
the highway north a southern road.
Goggle-eyed lamplights
blink uneven wattage
as the pulses
of your soulful heart.

I met a man who gave you bread
and meat and a warm bed
while you wrote *Black Boy,*
another who shared your Chicago loft;
some wait for released papers,
some salve old photographs.

A campus librarian near
Hollywood reads the unread
books to move with Bigger,
sees Mary's spittle as sperm
pushing her trunk,
holds the body as you hack her neck,
watches Bessie's downdraft
as a cross-corner shot.

That parable of black man, white woman,
the man's penis slung to his shin,
erect, foaming in that woman's womb,
the ambivalent female with smirk-shriek,
daylights of coitus stuck together,
through the nights the razored solution;
that the black man is nature,

the woman, on her drilled pedestal, divine,
the man with razor an artisan
in symmetry steel and sharp blades—
let him melt into this vat of precious metal,
let the female wipe her face of sperm,
let the black man's penis shrink to normal
service, let the posse eat their whips instead.

On the Seine I thought of you
on the towpath to Notre Dame;
at the Blue Note looking for Bud
on his *parisian thorofare;*
caught your blues from black musicians
while you died alone in prose;
some said you'd died of disconnection;
some said you dealt your own heartblow.

SPIRITUAL

Grandma's picket fence
balloon mask dancing
bloody moon on your black ribcage.

AFTERWORD: A FILM

Erect in the movies
with a new job,
Trader Horn
and *The Gay Woman*
unfold in a twinbill:
drums, wild dancing,
naked men, the silver
veils on the South Side.
He imagines nothing:
it is all before him,
born in a dream:
a gorilla broke loose
from his zoo
in a tuxedo: baboon.
You pick your red bottom.
The Daltons are the movies.

On my wall are pictures:
Jack Johnson, Joe Louis,
Harlow and Rogers:
"see the white god and die."

Underground I live in veils,
brick and cement,
the confession beaten out,
slung with hung carcasses,
a bloody cleaver grunting,
a dead baby in the sewer:
"all the people I saw were guilty."

Marked black I was shot,
double-conscious brother in the veil—
without an image of act or thought
double-conscious brother in the veil—

The rape: "Mrs. Dalton, it's me,
Bigger, I've brought Miss Dalton
home and she's drunk":
to be the idea in these minds,
double-conscious brother in the veil—
father and leader where is my king,
veils of kingship will lead these folks
double-conscious brother in the veil—
"see the white gods and die"
double-conscious brother in the veil—

From *Nightmare Begins Responsibility*
1975

"say it for two sons gone,
say nightmare, say it loud
panebreaking heartmadness:
nightmare begins responsibility"

Kin

When news came that your mother'd
smashed her hip, both feet caught
in rungs of the banquet table,
our wedding rebroken on the memory
of the long lake of silence
when the stones of her body
broke as an Irish fence of stones,
I saw your wet dugs drag
with the weight of our daughter
in the quick of her sleep
to another feeding;
then the shoulders dropped
their broken antenna branches
of fear at the knife
running the scars
which had been born into the colon
for the misspent enema,
the clubbed liver unclean
with the stones of the gall bladder,
and the broken arch of hip
lugging you to the lake,
the dough inner tube of lading
swollen with innerpatching.

I pick you up from the floor
of your ringing fears, the floor
where the photographs you have worked
into the cool sky of the gray you love,
and you are back at the compost pile
where the vegetables burn,
or swim in the storm of your childhood,

when your father egged you on with his
open machinery, the exhaust choking your sisters,
and your sisters choked still.

Now this voice stops you in accusation,
and the years pile up on themselves
in the eggs of your stretched sons,
one born on his birthday, both dead.
I pull you off into the sanctuary
of conciliation, of quiet tactics,
the uttered question, the referral,
which will quiet the condition you have seen
in your mother's shadow, the crutches
inching in the uncut grass,
and the worn body you will carry
as your own birthmark of his scream.

Landfill

Loads of trash and we light the match;
what can be in a cardboard box
can be in the bed of the pickup
and you jostle the containers onto the side road.
A match for this little road,
and a match for your son riding next to you firing,
and a match for the hole in the land filled with trees.
I will not mention concrete because theirs is the meshed
wire of concrete near the docks, and the concrete
of burned trees cut in cords of change-sawing,
and we will light a match in this too.

Work in anger for the final hour of adjustment
to the surveyors, and to the lawyers speaking of squatting,
and the land burning to no one.
This building of scrap metal, high as the storm that will break
it totally in the tornado dust,
and to the animals that have lived in the wheathay of their bedding
will beg for the cutting edge, or the ax,
or the electrified fencing that warms them in summer rain.

My son coughs on the tarred scrubble of cut trees,
and is cursed by the firelight, and beckoned to me to the pickup,
and washed of the soot of his sootskinned face,
and the dirt at the corners of my daughter's mouth will be trenchmouth;
and the worn moccasin of my woman will tear into the bulbed big toe,
and the blood will be black as the compost pile burning,
and the milk from her dugs will be the balm for the trenchmouth,
as she wipes her mouth from the smoke of the landfill filled with fire,
and these loads of trash will be the ashes for her to take:
and will be taken to the landfill, and filled, and filled.

Abe

"I lost my last name at Ellis Island"

When you came back after your heart
stalled on the Chinese steps,
what street name in Prague,
does not matter;
what matters is your song
of great strain in our 30's
called hard times,
when great men of art
were workers from breads
their mothers made to sell,
and when they ate
they laughed, and what cheese
they got they paid for twice
in the same day
to the same man;
what roads their fathers
walked for work
we'll never know.

What we know is the price
one pays for indifference,
the shoed nail bent
into each soul to kick
at the arched movement,
each yarmulke poised to crow
on your wife whose name
comes clear as the belled charge
of Coltrane we will listen
to in the room of your daughter,
her son the book
written as your heart
pours liquid fumes
of the life he must know,
and what the bread cost,
what you paid
to keep the stairwell
unchambered, unbypassed,
a red road open
at the crossroads
of scarred hands.

From a Town in Minnesota

"GUN: 'from the feminine in which both names mean WAR'"

One side tight in the case,
scope screwed on my head,
brown stock like my owner
unfiring, prepared;
bought from deadly shot
who went berserk in Newport,
I crept into Oakland
in a back seat
of a friend
who later gave up games
with dumdum shell
in his temple
but I was sleeping
on this top shelf
cuddled from explosion.

You want to borrow
me for a hunt
in Kenai,
and uncased
I loosen my handle
sight off center
tightening my strap
on your blade of flesh
I will hold on long
treks through berries
where the moose lie.

I go back to sleep
carried over frontiers
of clothing I lie among,
my master's grandfather
naked on the firing
range, his blue hat
broken at brim;
and know I will
awaken decades from here,
waiting for answers
that never speak to me,
cartridges
of an enemy
part stranger,
greased, armpit anchored,
waiting for the burned flit
of hair trigger
pulled toward the closet,
these skeletons I wear.

Black Cryptogram

When God
created
the black child
He was
showing off.

Grandfather

In 1915 my grandfather's
neighbors surrounded his house
near the dayline he ran
on the Hudson
in Catskill, N.Y.
and thought they'd burn
his family out
in a movie they'd just seen
and be rid of his kind:
the death of a lone black
family is *the Birth
of a Nation,*
or so they thought.
His 5'4" waiter gait
quenched the white jacket smile
he'd brought back from watered
polish of my father
on the turning seats,
and he asked his neighbors
up on his thatched porch
for the first blossom of fire
that would bring him down.

They went away, his nation,
spittooning their torched necks
in the shadows of the riverboat
they'd seen, posse decomposing;
and I see him on Sutter
with white bag from your
restaurant, challenged by his first
grandson to a foot-race
he will win in white clothes.

I see him as he buys galoshes
for his railed yard near Mineo's
metal shop, where roses jump
as the el circles his house
toward Brooklyn, where his rain fell;
and I see cigar smoke in his eyes,
chocolate Madison Square Garden chews
he breaks on his set teeth,
stitched up after cancer,
the great white nation immovable
as his weight wilts
and he is on a porch
that won't hold my arms,
or the legs of the race run
forwards, or the film
played backwards on his grandson's eyes.

Blackjack

1963;
we march.

I look out remedial
white windowed essays
from Pasadena
I will read tonight
and there you are visiting
three black sisters
excluded from official parade
"their skins unlovely."

Orange and Fair Oaks
to grow on
to the stadium
blocks where you stand
silent; I am silent—

Nodding I say
'47 high noon in the bleachers,
Cards in town,
you jog the outfield grass
lagging loose balls,
how you lofted their cream-
skinned signatures
over the white heads
where we sat pigeontoed
circling their dugout,
how we carried your curled
name to our table
while your team cursed

your singed garters
on pennant flagged tongues.

As they saw nothing
but your teeth and eyes
we saw the jeering train
unwinding its sheets in Georgia,
your mail cringing with snake
juice spat in the Bronx;
and when you crossed
our borders we cheered
our black ace
of the marked deck of Westwood,
the bowl we stand in,
the counter where their salted
nuts stack in their vacuum cans.

We will not speak of broad
jumps over tracks,
yardlines of pigskin
jaunted, stitched white balls
spiked at your skull:
we will remember the found
sleep and meals you lost
running over bases
their pitchers feared covering,
balls you made them eat
now flowering from your son's
funeral car.

High blood pressure,
diabetes,
your eyes gone blind,
I will not answer.
I steel home
at your back
down the red clay road
of their stadium
recalling Rachel,
my own daughter,
on deck.

"Did he say Blackie?"
my brother said
of the white boy
in row G:
"Black Jack,
the gamble's taken,
the debt unpaid,
and the answer,
answered, still to come."

for Jackie Robinson

Nightmare Begins Responsibility

I place these numbed wrists to the pane
watching white uniforms whisk over
him in the tube-kept
prison
fear what they will do in experiment
watch my gloved stickshifting gasolined hands
breathe *boxcar-information-please* infirmary tubes
distrusting white-pink mending paperthin
silkened end hairs, distrusting tubes
shrunk in his *trunk-skincapped*
shaven head, in thighs
distrusting-white-hands-picking-baboon-light
on his son who will not make his second night
of this wardstrewn intensive airpocket
where his father's asthmatic
hymns of *night-train,* train done gone
his mother can only know that he has flown
up into essential calm unseen corridor
going boxscarred home, *mamaborn, sweetsonchild*
gonedowntown into *researchtestingwarehousebatteryacid*
mama-son-done-gone/me telling her 'nother
train tonight, no music, no breathstroked
heartbeat in my infinite distrust of them:

and of my distrusting self
white-doctor-who-breathed-for-him-all-night
say it for two sons gone,
say nightmare, say it loud
panebreaking heartmadness:
nightmare begins responsibility.

Br'er Sterling and the Rocker

Any fool knows a Br'er in a rocker
is a boomerang incarnate; look at the blade
of the rocker, that wondrous crescent
rockin' in harness as poem.

To speak of poetry is the curled line straightened;
to speak of doubletalk, the tongue
gone pure, the stoic line a trestle
whistlin', a man a train comin' on:

Listen Br'er Sterling
steel-drivin' man, folk-said, folk-sayin',
that chair's a blues-harnessed star
turnin' on its earthly axis;

Miss Daisy, latch on that star's arc,
hold on sweet mama; Br'er Sterling's rocker glows.

for Sterling A. and Daisy T. Brown
June 16, 1973

Paul Laurence Dunbar: 1872–1906

One hundred years of headrags, bandages,
plantation tradition gone sour;
in the smokehouse, Newport, R.I.
a knotted metaphor collapsed in foyer,
Miss Ann finally understanding the elevator
where you sang your standard
imperfect lyrics.

Minstrel and mask:
a landscape of speech and body
burned in verbal space,
the match cinder unstandard:
double-conscious brother in the veil—
double-conscious brother in the veil:
double-conscious brother in the veil.

Corrected Review:
THEREISATREEMOREANCIENTTHANEDEN

"The tree is unique, qualitatively speaking, and cannot be subject to purely quantitative comparison; it is impossible to reduce the world of sense-perceptions to quantitative categories. Qualitative things do not belong to matter, which is merely mirror for it, so it can be seen, but not so that it can be altogether limited to the material plane."

"Man is created for the purpose of active participation in Divine Intellect, of which he is the central reflection."

From the *source* comes the imagery and language,
compassion and complexity in the *one*
achieved in the imagination conjured,
admired in surrender and transcendence:
where is the *perfect* man?

Words beyond words to conjure this malaise
to infamy and death in effort
immanence forsaken:
to blow the music
maelstrom-tempered.

Our mode is our jam session
of tradition,
past in this present moment
articulated, blown through
with endurance,
an unreaching extended
improvised love of past masters,
instruments technically down:

structured renderings of reality
our final war with self;

rhetoric/parlance arena-word-consciousness:
morality: man to man
man to god
in a tree
more ancient than eden.

for Leon Forrest

Alice

"The word made stone, the stone word"
"A RITE is an action the very form of which is the result of a Divine
Revelation."

1

You stand waist-high in the snakes
beating the weeds for the gravebed
a quarter mile from the nearest
relative, an open field in Florida: lost,
looking for Zora, and when she speaks
from her sunken chamber to call
you to her side, she calls
you her distant cousin, her sister
come to mark her burial place
with bright black stone.
She has known you would do this—
her crooked stick, her straight lick—
and the lie you would have to tell
to find her, and that you lied
to her relatives in a conjure-riddle
of the words you have uttered,
calling her to communion.

A black rock of ages you have placed
where there was no marker,
and though the snakes abound
in this preserve from ancestral space,
you have paid your homage
in traditional line, the face open:
your face in the woman-light of surrender
toughened in what you were.

2

Floods of truth flow from your limbs
of these pages in a vision swollen
in experience and pain:
that child you stepped into blossom
of a man's skull beaten into smile
of submission, you gathering horse nectar
for offering over a baby's crusted gasp,
for centuries of motherhood and atonement
for which you write, and the rite written.

And for this I say your name: Alice,
my grandmother's name, your name,
conjured in snake-infested field
where Zora Neale welcomed you home,
and where I speak from now
on higher ground of her risen
black marker where you have written
your name in hers, and in mine.

for Alice Walker

From *Images of Kin*
1977

Can't you see
what love and heartache's done to me
I'm not the same as I used to be
this is my last affair

Crossing Lake Michigan

The amp light on the station
wagon has just gone out;
we climb up the hatch-stairs
to the deck, the clouds mildewed
as storms move east, bucketing
the interstate with torrential rain.
The ferry bucks my daughter's soft
forehead into my neck, dreaming,
perhaps of strawberry patches
she investigates for bright
spots ripening as she skips
the white; late one August evening
she appeared lost for hours
as storm clouds rocked
in rowboats moving in swirls
of leaves under lakeside elms;
when she was discovered, her rear-
end skyward, bent, we foraged for pure
red signals of strawberry.

I brush her hair back from her face
so similar to my sister's at the same age,
smile, though I overhear two Michigan
tourists, returning home, talk of menace
of cities, how King asked for glory
of newsprint and ate the balcony railing
in conspiracy of his lost appetite;

I think of amp lights that will ignite
our three darkened hours to Ann Arbor,
a call made to an all-night self-service
garage where you can buy parts.

She wakes with songs learned from her teacher,
her mother trailing a lawnmower of seeds
on the furrowed lawn, catching the tune
of a great thrush lock-stepped in imitation.
His one song of politics, the power of the ferry
climbing swells to a future of hungry birds
lost in Michigan, where a strike wavers near a highway
I will go by: she will ask for the strawberry's whiteness,
and why men will not eat at her table of red,
and what song to sing to vacationers returning to Michigan.

Tongue-Tied in Black and White

"I had a most marvelous piece of luck. I died."

In Los Angeles
while the mountains cleared of smog
your songs dreamed
Jefferson and Madison
walking hand in hand
as my grandfather walked to Canada.
What eyes met the black student
next to me, her hands fanning
your breezy neck from this veranda,
but Henry's/Mr. Bones.

Home from Mexico and you in LIFE,
I walk dead center into the image
of LBJ cloistered by the draping
flags of Texas and the confederacy,
and as my aunt of Oklahoma told me
I understood your father's impulse
to force you into Crane's nightmare.

After the Roethke reading in Seattle
you stroked the stout legs of an ex-
student's wife while he sketched
you in adoration and as you cautioned
your audience, "forty-five minutes and no longer,"
how Harvard paid in prestige not money,
how a man at Harvard read for four hours,
that he ought to be set down in the Roman
courtyard and have rocks set upon him
until death—your audience laughed.

You admired my second living son
as you loved the honeyed dugs of his mother,
your spotless tan suit weaving in the arch
where goalposts supported you in foyer
for you would not fall.

At your last public reading,
let out for fear of incident without a drink,
your foot bandaged from fire you'd
stamped out in a wastebasket of songs,
your solitary voice speckled in Donne,
in Vermont where the stories of Bread
Loaf, Brown, another broken leg abandoned
in monotones of your friends studying you;

Now I must take up our quarrel:
never dangerous with women
though touched by their nectared hair,
you wrote in that needful black idiom
offending me, for only your inner voices
spoke such tongues, your father's soft prayers
in an all black town in Oklahoma; your ear lied.
That slave in you was white blood forced to derision,
those seventeenth-century songs saved you from review.

Naked, in a bottle of Wild Turkey,
the bridge you dived over was your source:
St. Paul to St. Louis to New Orleans,
the *asiento,* Toussaint, border ruffians,
signature of Lincoln, porters bringing
messages to white widows of Europe,
a classics major, and black, taking your classes,
the roughpage of your bird legs and beard
sanitizing your hospital room,
the last image of your bandaged foot
stamping at flames on the newborn bridge.

This is less than the whole truth
but it is the blacker story
and what you asked to be told:
"lay off the sauce when you write"
you said to me, winking at the brownskinned
actress accompanying me to the lectern;
and how far is Texas from Canada
and our shared relatives in blacktown
on the outskirts of your tongue, tied still.

Healing Song

He stoops down eating sunflowers
snowballed at his prayer-rugged
table, "message/solution/masses"
his ghetto-blues-plantation,
driven into inner/outer realities
as buffers drawn from his eyes.

Penned in that magnificent voice
where *victorola* mutters "Koppin" songs,
his sedge burning night-trains,
this serape-man found wanting
only in that "God Don't Like Ugly"
phrase; he draws his own lightning,
believing differently,
an angel surrendering angles of desire:
his masked heart-centered soul reveals.

Rused in dance steps of jubilo,
atavisms of worship shutting out sound,
his full essential flowering
balances in the 4 A.M. traduction,
his Emancipation Tree.

Hidden in ancient tetters
of autobiography,
he tropes of 1863 *moverings,*
his Osceolas already sacrificed
as Lincoln's mass production lines
funnel bodies to the Crater;
his Easter families agonize
at blue doors of transformation.

Self-accused in venial sins, his gorgeous
offerings lift blind pigs to Bessie's
witchdoctoring, her blue-black tongue
singing down Jesus,
"watch your goin' be like comin' back,"
he witnesses flesh pull down in anger,
killing calves of hunger to no higher law.

Ragboned Bob Hayden, shingled in slime,
reaches for his cereus ladder of midnight flight,
his seismographic heartbeats
sphinctered in rhiney polygraphs of light;
Dee-troit born and half-blind
in diction of arena and paradise,
his ambient nightmare-dreams streak his tongue;
mementos of his mother, of Erma, he image-makes
peopling the human family of God's mirror,
mingling realities, this creature of transcendence
a love-filled shadow, congealed and clarified.

UPLIFT FROM A DARK TOWER

"Those who profess to favor Freedom, and yet deprecate agitation, are men who want crops without plowing up the ground. . . . Power concedes nothing without a demand."
—Frederick Douglass

"Because in a day when the human mind aspired to a science of human action, a history and psychology of the mighty effort of the mightiest century, we fell under the leadership of those who would compromise with truth in the past in order to make peace in the present and guide policy in the future."
—W. E. B. Du Bois

"The presentation of facts, on a high, dignified plane, is all the begging that most rich people care for. . . . It is easily possible that some of my former owners might be present to hear me speak."
—Booker T. Washington

THE BATTLE OF SARATOGA
(SPRINGS) REVISITED

Just when I think I've got you nailed
to your cross of uplift
I see your name in the private printing
of a history of *Yaddo,*
meaning "shadow" or "shimmering,"
its five-hundred-acre testimonial to lakes
over gardens, trees
buried with *lost* children
whose memory donated this tower
studio to my writing of you.

Outside the door might lie *Etienne,*
the cannibal brought by missionaries
from Africa to be trained for service
in the experimental summer of 1881.
He would be St. Patrick to Yaddo's Ireland
handling snakes, woodland spiders,
as simple playthings, his station
outside this room, asleep at threshold,
his carving knife, guarding me safely from exit.
Such loyalty, devotion might lie in
pure strain of his cannibal ancestry:
"my body may be black but my soul is white."

He went back to Africa as a trader.

DINING FROM A TREED CONDITION,
AN HISTORICAL SURVEY

"in order to be successful in any kind of undertaking, I think the main
thing is for one to grow to the point where he completely forgets himself;
that is, to lose himself in a great cause."

At the dinner table where you sat with Peabody,
stirred by the shrewd handicap of scholars and savants,
you opened your certain ginger face
"I was born a slave," rolling jordanized,
accomplished in freedom of all pride,
of all bitterness of a handicapped race
made really safe from Democracy,
the *Trask* check slipped in loamed black
cloth in many dinner wallets of conversation.

I look out the tower window over the sun-dial
of Etienne's savage memory carved in blue spruce
and the rainbowed cypress hearing Christmas prayers
of Barhyte's slaves, Thom Campbell, his wife, Nancy,
quartered in clear pieces of Bear Swampground
southeast of the Rose Garden, conjuring amused
comic tales of Tom Camel's unselfish episodes
of tree-climbing and masquerade.

Told to saw off a limb on Mr. White's place
he sat on the limb vigorously sawing the obstructing
branch; dazed after a loud crack, on the ground
Tom cried to Mr. White: "Oh, no Sah! I had the good
fortune to land on mah head";
dressed up in carriage, in woman's clothes,
Camel posed as Burr's Mistress in Stone's
"Reminiscences of Saratoga," as Madame Jumel on one of her
visits in 1849, in *criminal* intimacy, at US Hotel,
threatened, bribed, as she followed her counterfeit
double, Tom Camel, fanning himself, curtseying
to crowds on every side to the lakefront with Burr.
(Poor Hamilton never had a chance at masquerade;
Burgoyne, Benedict Arnold cavort on Saratoga field.)

Tales of remembrance, of master and slave,
of mistress, of American patriot in the French style,
take me through statuary, rock and rose gardens,
lakes named for children, concola, white pines
as "spiritual linguist," the shadow of Yaddo's
pine and rose on the thresholds of cypress, the hanging tree
where Mohawks worshipped
and Camel's chained image swung to ground,
a head injury of couffered masquerade.

The caned walking stick
I borrow from bicycle paths
in metaphor for your whipping to early death,
inviting Madame Jumel perhaps,
your huge clothesbasket full of checks,
the *exposition* address
marketed in cottonballs of fleeced gowns
in a dining hall
where the surprise party
was held on the burned ashes of this rainbow.

THE FOUNDING FATHERS IN PHILADELPHIA

"some of the questions he asked about the Negro church denominations were: the number of communicants, the percentage of male and female members, the seating capacity of the churches, the value of the parsonages, and the total collection of the African Methodist Episcopal Missionary Department from 1904 to 1908. Again, there was no connection drawn between any of the material offered in 1909 and the data given in the earlier v's."

Meeting in secret, with my great
grandfather AME bishop in Philadelphia,
just before his debarking the ship
for South Africa, I see the choices
for education and literacy of a *downtrodden* people
flushed down the outlet of the ocean
liner, where my earmarked greatgrand
fluxed precious diamonds from the Zulu
chiefs, before stolen by customs.

What tongues did the diamonds speak?
To be educated by black spiritual linguists
from runaway Canada
or the pontiffs of paternity
in the plazas of Saratoga,
I remind myself with a visit to harnessed
racing, no single black jockey present,
for this is even betting handicapped
at fifty dollars and my best thoroughbred
in August, where the Indian spirits
praise a five-hundred-year-old tree
nourished by sacred spring water,
its radioactivity signs ignored,
the freed slave runaways
paddling down the Hudson to Catskill
to the dayline my grandfather ran
before the bridge to Kingston
took his house, his children, to Brooklyn.

PSYCHOPHOTOS OF HAMPTON

". . . in all fairness to Washington we must recall that Armstrong, in effect,
gave Washington his career."
—Robert B. Stepto

Dining at 8 and 6:30
with a lunchpail for noon,
I type out the echoes of artist
in the high studio of the tower,
blackened in the image of Etienne,
his cannibal ancestry sharpened
by the sloped Adirondacks toward Montreal
where French/Indian alliances of beaver pelts
end in burrows of buffalo on open plains,
another mountain range to cross, the salt lick
of lake claiming runaway bigamists,
and the great Sioux herds on the run to Cody,
named for the diseased man who died in Denver,
his widow offered forty grand to be buried near his name.

On a ride down 9W to Esopus, New York,
where Wiltwyck boys from five boroughs
came to the Roosevelt mansion-estate, the volunteers
driving buses with Mennonite alms, to home visits
of abandoned projects, each welfare roll breaking
in fired windows, I take the granite sites
of General Armstrong into view, his great twin
burial rocks, Vermont granite, Sandwich lava
entrancing the mausoleum of the great divide
of history, of railroad lands, of the *Dakotah*,
Sandwich missions, the uplift of schoolmarms
tuning the pens of the Freedmen's Bureau toward
the thin line of train track near Emancipation Tree.

At $68/head, the great Dakotah nation went to college,
from Black Hills to mosquitoed swamp near Fort Monroe,
where the fevered zeal of the government
reimbursed each Indian with black suit,
haircut, and a class photograph:

I walk out over swampgrounds, campsites,
drumbeats of the great cemetery
surrounded by sane spirits of the great mansion
at Arlington where Robert E. Lee's doorstep
sprouted with Union graves terraced from his veranda:

For Daniel Fire-Cloud, Sioux, South Dakotah
died September 3 1886, 14 years
Armstrong Firecloud, Sioux, born Hampton
died August 6 1886 infant
Virginia Medicine-Bull, Sioux, South Dakotah
died January 30 1886
Simon Mazakutte, Sioux, South Dakotah
died March 26 1884, 18 years
Benjamin Bear-Bird, Sioux, South Dakotah
died August 4 1885, aged 2 years
Edith Yellow-Hair, Sioux, South Dakotah
died November 26 1885, aged 8 years
Emma Whips, Sioux, South Dakotah
died March 25 1885
Lora Bowed-Head Snow, Sioux, South Dakotah
died March 20 1885, aged 22 years
Mary Pretty-Hair, Sioux, South Dakotah
died January 6 1885, aged 14 years
Eva Good-Road, Sioux, South Dakotah
died January 4, 1884, aged 17 years
Belany Sayon-Sululand, South Africa
died December 10 1884, aged 22 years
Edward Buck, Sioux, South Dakotah
died May 30 1884, aged 17 years
Croaking Wing, Mandan, North Dakotah
died April 21 1884, aged 17 years
Francesca Rios, Papago, Arizona
died August 21 1883, aged 15 years

Henry Kendall Acolehut, Yuma, Arizona
died August 13 1883, aged 22 years
Tasute White Back, Gros Ventre, North Dakotah
died January 24 1882, aged 15 years.
I leave out fully anglicized names,
some duplications among the Sioux (meaning dog)
for fear of repeat of the Dakotah.
Buried in graveyards of the great founding
academies, their souls finally saved
from highlands where they were born.
The great Lincoln train
winds into great centennial avenues
where each kneeled slave has the great veil
lifted from his eyes, his enlightened
face literate from heart to mind,
penciled in nightmare,
where the rainbow mansion,
tiered rose garden, Bearground Swamp
vessels the dark interior
of this book I write of the Shadow,
Unjungian and unsurveyed,
in the cleaning of your first bedroom,
over and over the coaldust you brought
under fingernails
as you scratched toward the caning
which would take your exhibition,
your address of the great ship,
its crew calling for water,
clear-watered-buckets-scooping-downward
in five equally broken fingers.

Separate as the limed hand
the five great Indian nations
disappear along the Trail
of Tears, the common man of Andrew
Jackson looking moonstruck in black regiments
for the Seminoles of Florida,
each Catholic outpost
St. Paul's Reservation of Little Crow

waiting for rations,
the St. Louis Fair
where Geronimo breathed the gas
from the Ford caught in the mud
gatewayed in his western eyes,
to New Orleans, where the musicians
stomp all night to Buster's for breakfast,
the buildings boarded up with slave anklets,
the militia protecting the war ships
of Toussaint in Napoleon's gift to Jefferson.

Your simplest image was the crab-barrel,
each black hand pulling the escaping soul
back into the pit where the turpentine
gangs sang, cutting their way through each
wilderness, each Indian amulet dropping
in cross-fires of settlers,
your great dining hall opening:
"I was born a slave,"
countered by Aristotle's
"some men are natural born slaves,"
in the boards of Wall Street,
where Melville wrote the dark glimmerings
scrimshaw tales, attached by the whale,
his bludgeoned knife raised in combat,
his sweat in the oiled battle with self,
where the nation stormed in fish beds
as laughing men and women dove
in triangular trade winds.

The last view is the best,
from the terrace overhang,
with a toothbrush,
seeing rock gardens and roses
pool in cascading fountains:
the Renaissance built on slave trading,
Etienne proud of his lineage,
Booker T's bookings humbled his beginnings,
the abstract masks giving off power,

its conjured being dynamized in my skin,
reminiscing at the founder's table
where the talk was of politics,
rhetoric, and the literature of the great
rainbowed swamp from the vision of the black tower.

From *Healing Song for the Inner Ear*
1985

The first true phrase sings out in barnyard;
the hunt in books for quail.

Double Elegy

Whatever city or country road
you two are on
there are nettles,
and the dark invisible
elements cling to your skin
though you do not cry
and you do not scratch
your arms at forty-five degree angles
as the landing point of a swan
in the Ohio, the Detroit River;

at the Paradise Theatre
you named the cellist
with the fanatical fingers
of the plumber, the exorcist,
and though the gimmickry at wrist
and kneecaps could lift the séance
table, your voice was real
in the gait and laughter of Uncle
Henry, who could dance on either
leg, wooden or real, to the sound
of the troop train, megaphone,
catching the fine pitch of a singer
on the athletic fields of Virginia.

At the Radisson Hotel,
we once took a fine angel
of the law to the convention center,
and put her down as an egret
in the subzero platform of a friend—
this is Minneapolis, the movies
are all of strangers, holding themselves

in the delicacy of treading water,
while they wait for the trumpet
of the Twentieth Century Limited
over the bluff or cranny.
You two men like to confront
the craters of history and spillage,
our natural infections of you
inoculating blankets and fur,
ethos of cadaver and sunflower.

I hold the dogwood blossom,
eat the pear, and watch the nettle
swim up in the pools
of the completed song
of Leadbelly and Little Crow
crooning the buffalo and horse
to the changes and the bridge
of a twelve-string guitar,
the melody of "Irene";
this is really good-bye—
I can see the precious stones
of embolism and consumption
on the platinum wires of the mouth:
in the flowing rivers, in the public baths
of Ohio and Michigan.

News from Fort Ancient

Don't ask me now, Jim Wright,
why this place comes to mind
but it is not arrowhead imagery
I look for, and the Indian burial mounds
embanked against the swivel and pull
of the Little Miami
won't bring you back to Ohioan
in this life, your soft glottals
and dirty jokes forever lost
in the atmosphere of swans
however dead and the oil leaks
from the cavity of the larynx
and lungs from which you sang.

You could cover it with platinum
but the satchel grew heavy
in translation: Chinese,
old German, a quaint, greasy Yiddish,
Spanish jazz, even from the mountains
of Cesar Vallejo,
even from the lips of Coltrane,
the breakaway backbone dice of Little Crow.

I knew a horse that did not sing
at the nearest corner post
in a field full of alfalfa;
he knew he didn't belong there
and so did I; I took the udder
of meat that hung from the mane
of Crazy Horse and made his enchantment,
an OM-2 automatic,

and the lake stood still in the early silt
of morning, without a fish, or a bird
in sight.
        You and Annie did walk
over a few blocks to the Y
to hear Etheridge and me read
in a blizzard—and you walked
back to the den of a world
out West; Cincinnati comes to mind
only because I went three deceptive
times to the bureau of health
to find out where a friend's mother was buried.

She died in 1937 and knew a few Cheyenne
in Oklahoma: when she picketed for social
justice she went to jail—the certificate
says she died of *tuberculosis of the hip,*
an impossible illness; at Hillcrest Cemetery
the locks lock even before entrance,
and the phone rings to no answer even in the snow.

You know why I am standing on the Ohio
River, right next to an FM jazz station,
which ought to be on stilts, but is on a raft
bobbing on the windward side of a good restaurant.
I could see your suckhole if you held still
a little longer so we could build
your burial mound close enough to the edge
to be washed away forever.

In Hayden's Collage

Van Gogh would paint the landscape
green—or somber blue;
if you could see the weather
in Amsterdam in June, or August,
you'd cut your lobe too,
perhaps simply on heroin,
the best high in the world,
instead of the genius of sunflowers,
blossoming trees. The Japanese
bridge in Hiroshima,
precursor to the real impression,
modern life, goes to Windsor, Ontario,
or Jordan, or the Natchez
Trace. From this angle, earless,
a torsioned Django Rhinehart
accompanies Josephine. You know
those rainbow children couldn't
get along in this *ole worl'*.

Not over that troubled water;
and when the band would play once
too often in Arkansas, or Paris,
you'd cry because the sunset was too
bright to see the true colors,
the first hue, and so nearsighted
you had to touch the spiderman's
bouquet; you put your arcane colors
to the spatula and cook
to force the palate in the lion's
den—to find God in all the light
the paintbrush would let in—
the proper colors,

the corn, the wheat, the valley,
dike, the shadows, and the heart
of self—minnow of the universe,
your flaccid fishing pole,
pieced together, never broken, never end.

The Loon

The estate bird
sits on the water
outside my window;
if you watch long
enough you will see
her dive
from her canopy,
and in the understory
of the weather,
in trees,
beneath the surface,
you might see another
estate bird.

In this scene the call
goes out to the ground cover,
where you can lay your face,
unbroken by the ceremonial
tears of the funeral,
on ferns.

Oh deciduous pouch
of awful leaves
at a would-be cemetery,
listen to the loon.

You could dream conifers,
the deep roots of burrowing
animals and insects,
the opossum
drunk on his tail
hearing the interior voice
of secret soil layer
where we bury her.

Camp Story

I look over the old photos
for the US Hotel fire,
1900 Saratoga Springs,
where your grandfather
was chef on loan
from Catskill
where you were born.

The grapes from his arbor
sing in my mouth:
the smoke from the trestle
of his backyard,
the engine so close
to the bedroom
I can almost touch it,
make bricks from the yards
of perfection,
the clear puddles from the Hudson River,
where you would make change
at the dayline,
keep the change from the five
Jack "Legs" Diamonds would leave
on the counter top or the stool.

Where is the CCC camp
you labored in
to send the money home to the family,
giving up your scholarship
so you could save the family
homestead from the banks of the river.

All across America the refugees
find homes in these camps
and are made to eat
at a table of liberty
you could have had
if you could not spell
or count, or keep time.

I see you, silent, wordfully
talking to my brother, Jonathan,
as he labors on the chromatic
respirator; you kiss his brown
temple where his helmet left
a slight depression
near a neat line of stitches
at the back of his skull.

As he twitches to chemicals
the Asian nurses catheter
into the cavities and caves
of his throat and lungs:
the doctor repeats the story
of his chances.

The Drowning of the Facts of a Life

Who knows why we talk of death
this evening, warm beyond the measure
of breath; it will be cool tomorrow
for in the waters off Long Beach
my brother's ashes still collect
the flowers of my mother and father,
my sister dropped in the vase
of a face they made of old places,
the text of water.

Tonight we talk of losses in the word
and go on drowning in acts of faith
knowing so little of humility,
less of the body,
which will die in the mouth of reality.

This foolish talk in a country
that cannot pronounce napalm
or find a path to a pool of irises
or the head of a rose.

My brother was such a flower;
he would spring into my path
on a subway train, above the ground
now, on the way home from school,
letting the swift doors pinch
his fingers of books and records,
house supplies from the corner market,
as he leaped back to the station
platform, crying his pleasure
to his brother,
who was on the train . . .

getting off at next exit
to look for him.

This is how we make our way home:
Each day when the Amtrak express
on the northeast corridor
takes my heritage from Boston
to the everglades of Maryland,
I think of the boy who sat
on the platform in the Canarsie,
on the uneven projects of New Lots
Avenue, BMT:

he was so small he could slip
through the swinging chains
of the express train
on the Williamsburg Bridge,
and not get touched by the third rail,
the chain link fencing of the accordion
swiveling to the swing and curses
of the motorman.

A fortnight my brother lay in coma,
his broken pate and helmet
in a shopping bag of effects,
his torn-off clothes and spattering
coins, the keys to the golden Yamaha—
with remnants of pavement in his scalp,
the trace of jacket laid under his head,
the black Continental idling
at anchor with the infinite,
the same black ice of the subway.

I came to chant over his fungus-
eaten flesh, allergic to his own
sweat, sweeter than the women
and children collecting
in caravan behind him; the Asian
nurses, so trained in the cadence
of thermometer and brain scan,

came in their green bracelets
and uniforms to relieve him—
a catheter of extract
makes the pomade of his hair
disappear, for his lips twitch
in remembrance at impact,
rage at the power of love,
the welcome table and the tabernacle
for his broken shoes and helmet.

Ponder the spent name of Jonathan,
apple and brother in the next
world, where the sacred text
of survival is buried in the bosom
of a child, radiated
in moonlight forever.
I touch the clean nostril
of the body in his mechanical
breathing, no chant sound enough
to lift him from the rest
of contraption
to the syncopated dance of his name.

Pullman Pass

He was eighty-seven
when I photographed
him, straight up
in the natural light
of his fifty-year
gold service Pullman's
pass, Twentieth Century Limited,
and claimed he was there
when Rockefeller and Vanderbilt
agreed on the merger
at the US Hotel
in Saratoga Springs;
he'd been a jockey then—
the Skidmore girls
would count the hairs
on his smooth skin
while he told them stories
in any direction or position.

He told this dime story
once about Rockefeller
giving out new dimes
in the parlor car
relaxing from his dinner.

"I'll put these with the others,"
Henry said to Rockefeller;
"How many of those do you have?"
and so Henry went back to his locker
and brought back a cigar
box with a rubber band around it,
and opened up the lid.

Rockefeller turned to his lawyer-
accountant and said to count
the dimes in the box
and write out the check
for the amount,
a dollar for a dime.

Henry had a soft voice;
he roadsided every cavern
and watering hole when he rode
on his pass;
                    he bought his wife
a farm with that Rockefeller
check: $2600,
a lot of acreage
for a black man
who feigned reading and writing;
straight back, tall as an arrow,
and pretty walking out the US
Hotel, where he had friends.

Segregated then at the Hotel:
wouldn't let no white people work there.

Horse-Trading

He was accomplished on eight instruments,
none of them the women he loved,
and his middle son changed his name
to his mother's
the result of a quarrel.

You cradled him in your uniform
cut down from your unit measure
of paratrooper's boots,
for you were not coming home
in your thin quarterback
arms you once had broken
in preseason scrimmage
so you did not got to high school
or sue, or break out of the *I Am
Movement* your mother ladled
on her Irish brow.

So what of your perfect pitch,
the prosody of a mixed marriage,
same formality and freedom,
your cocksmanlike posturing,
flat feet going nowhere
in the open field
except for the snowing over,
the blanket, the foxhole, the spun reeds:

Once you thought Madison Square Garden
was a real garden with roses;
saved by the bell
your father did not die for nothing.

Hooking

Just about ready for medicare
and limping on that bum leg
nobody'd know you could mix
fine woolens from Australia,
spot-dyed into songs of the knead—
hook your way to the carpeted
gallery of birds and flowers.
The oak leaf breaks into difficulties,
pansies, their simplicity of touch
even at the water's edge,
as close to where you were born
as Newfoundland—
                    your man's gone
fourteen years, and in six
days you'll be sixty-five,
                            running the best
kitchen in Saratoga,
                    forty pails
in the early light,
                    gray hours
of days off where you sit over the burlap
backing of the great rugs you push
into deceits of gold, rouge, gabardine—

Your birthplace is so far north, eight
hours beyond St. John, you can't go home,
though your father sits in his blindness,
walking the caverns of the family house
alone in his deafness; even the phone
can't make him walk any faster than your hook.

I can't ask you whether some Spanish flu
in 1920 made you limp,
left you childless, but I know your brother
drowned, and that your husband could leap
into the eggs of the mosquito without a single
drink, hitch from the hooking eye
you made for him.
                              Nothing stands up forever;
your cane hangs on the wall just by the stairs;
when you come down you lift it as staff
to the rich life you sustain—
                                        the music of the race-
track is clear in the mist and humidity
of August—West House closes at Christmas,
and this year you have ten days without a single
break from the hook and pattern of the winter's
sun. East is the best house; the flowers
bend in fragrance of the feed you lay
out for the cardinal who stays all year.
Since the sea is your favorite image in handiwork
as thistle and harp of the seamstress,
haven of the great maps of the world,
right under your foot, the heart stamps upon us—
stump, the pulling out of mistakes,
in the candelabra of your hair.

Stepto's Veils

I'm not blaming anyone either,
but authorial control is a reality,
does lie within the nexus of race,
and elsewhere also; upstairs,
where the saints carouse, upper
registers of song, encounters
on the levee, and in the stratospheres
of Coleman Hawkins—broken on his own wings.
I love the landing of a crippled bird,
all by himself in any key,
the glittering keyboard of a cartoon
character's teeth scattered into a dice
game. The confrontations of the word
are like the grace notes, and if you add
a race ritual or two, no harm
in epiphanies, the private jokes of cages,
arena and the mask of minstrelsy,
folk songs underneath the stars.

You pull back the cotton batting
of the great traditions, such privacy
and showmanship not only on the baseball
field, or in the segregated corners
of the dance halls; I thought I saw you
in a cummerbund, tuxedo junction
and the white gloves of Bert Williams,
who used to court my grandmother
while riding horse down Fifth Avenue,
same avenue our ancestors went down
going and coming from France.

I think of Thomas Jefferson's foray
into the black section of Marseilles,
storing up footnotes for the Louisiana
Purchase, and since land is personal
the myth of Haiti and the Citadel.
Which brings me to veils: the doctor
would sit in his armchair making notes
to the arpeggios of the world;
finding no text completely comfortable,
he shook out his spats, smoked his last
Benson & Hedges, checked the stairwell
where he kept his piece, then went out
on maneuvers in the midlands of the people.
The buildings there were less than grand;
there were holes in the canebrake,
but the doctor had good eyesight,
saw the swamp and campground, heard the music:
the trouble with this century is more than history;
as for intertextualities:
this year's for Charlie Parker,
born sixty years ago in August,
died my senior year in high school—
nobody knew his tunes where I ate my lunch
with the sansei boys just out of camp.

The Body Polity

A half-century ago the Scottsboro Boys
jackknifed into vectors of the runagate
dream, and not the dream of Anglican
vice, when act hid shadow, shadow act.

Decatur relatives and neighbors
not too far from Chehaw Station and Tuskegee,
flight squadrons and turkey regiments
peopled medical corps, jim crow'd tuxedo junction.

I saw the oldest son of any slave hide his thought
in Latin-English treasury books of Apuleius,
saw the roots of Constitution and the family Bible,
tree and joist of history, and the self: democracy.

A sterling beacon tintype or a work song;
thumbed eight-ball English, elegiac blues, on any continental shelf.

The Pen

"The artifact is the completion of personality."

The Big E. is still making up
complexity;
                    he can't be stolen
from—his long black tongue
isn't nearly as deadly
                    as his memory
which is of the frontier,
the fiber and floor covering,
the blossom and elixir of bhang
and hashish, and the pen is quick:
the seeds are used as food for caged birds

and so the Big E. enjoys a shared delight,
a feast.

The Big E. don't like theft—
he got powerful arms, a scarred
eyelid, and a pocketknife
that has a fast safety and a quick release—
it has a double-edged sword,
                    it is as black
as gunpowder, as red as a hieroglyphic
rose; the Big E. is a gangplank
with nettles on either side
                    the berry sweet
enough for the nightingale to eat,
jam of the crow.
                    The Big E. has orchestration—
his patterns of the word fling out into destiny

as a prairie used to when the Indians
were called Kiowa, Crow, Dakota, Cheyenne.

The Big E. ain't in love with Indian-hating;
he don't like phony dance—he's got his problems
with terrain in Mississippi—
                                        the great slab
of stone in Mississippi makes you swim—
The Big E. likes hawks;
                                he's got time for deer—
he can seed watermelon, pumpkins, cantaloupe—
he got problems with theft,
                                highway robbery—
his own name—and he likes the source
of things, deeds, and the snakeskin well-wrought
and finely earned; he likes the sentiment
of defanging—he got two teeth with poison
in between, got a hot, tested lip,
                                a sense of ease
at the break—he's got a tinker bell
likes radio equipment, got tapes in his closet,
old coats still in style from the haberdashery
shop—has a sense of honor on the dance floor.
don't step on nobody's feet, brings his own smoke,
can tan a hide, fish in the stream of the dream,
the big dream—looks for the possible in things
unwritten; and when it comes to rite, jokes, jokes bad!

"Goin' to the Territory"

"The prayers of both could not be answered—that of neither has been
answered fully."
—Abraham Lincoln

Ethical schizophrenia you called it:
come back to haunt the cattle-drive,
Indians coming into blacktown
because it's home; your father's will
lies uncontested, his blood welling up in oil;
"Deep Second" hones its marks in Jimmy Rushing;
Charlie Christian's father leads the blind.

Such instruments arrange themselves
at Gettysburg, at Chickamauga;
the whites in Tulsa apologize
in the separate library,
all the books you dreamed of,
fairy tales and Satchmo jesting
to the Court of St. James,
infirmary is the saints already home.

The hip connected to the thigh
converges in tuberculosis; your mother's
knees spank the planks of rectory,
your father's image sanctified
in documents, in acts won out
on hallelujahs of "A" train,
nine Scottsboro Boys spun upward
over thresholds of Duke's dance.

Dance and mask collect their greasepaint,
idioms stand on bandstand, in stove-
pipe pants of a riverman, in gambling shoes,
his gold-toothed venom vexing sundown,
the choir at sunrise-service cleansing
a life on a jim crow funeral car.

The first true phrase sings out in barnyard;
the hunt in books for quail.

MY BOOK ON TRANE

you lived or died on your instrument,
you died or lived on your instrument.

when we went to Japan
I prayed at the shrine
for the war dead broken
at Nagasaki;

BANDSTAND

Monk's dissonant hat
willing every change of direction;
all those influences in your head
touching the wrong target—
none of this recorded,
the ears of the kitchen painted black,
all the musicians in common clothes,
dressing for the ancestors.

You learned to appreciate the pews,
the cooling iron,
the cooling board where the bodies,
guns in the recording studios,
became the tuning forks,
meals eaten while running in place
for Mother and Dad
who could dance.

ARPEGGIOS

Hawks and pigeons first
on the jacket leaving profiles
of pressed flowers
on conked hair;
favorite compositions, things
distinguished in the pennywhistles
of the prow
in the mines.

Even in Rio, Paris,
little tangible is edible
that doesn't choke in the gullet
of misery,
hungry men playing
for each other,
blocking out this criminal world.

Genius lost and found
on the corners of Soweto;
Miriam, alone in her palatial
campus suite, clicking the sermon,
Armageddon the village-veld.

POLLS

Some bloods can't count and won't vote;
imagine Desmond ahead of Trane
on the wrong instrument.
—I'm not saying Desmond can't play—
but *Playboy* was embarrassed,
sounding like swing all over again:
whuhfolks creating jazz—best records in the world
being sold under the counter;
Miles's soundtrack for a movie
only ten inches wide.

Trane created a freak show;
everybody scared he wouldn't salute
the old musicians,
the women of salutation,
his mother, cousin, wife,
the best connections
from the kitchen to the best restaurants.

Some knew such playing
is possible
only when you're ready to die.

Most whites always keeping score,
making it too easy to find the way,
guaranteeing you'll never feel loss,
black and white on paper,
in the ground.

SOLO

Only sweet in the middle registers,
the fluegelhorn making a new band
music, each cadenza
his solo of spare parts.

Signing the contract, unhinged
in the voice box, each triplet
measured in uniformed police,
he prayed for the big horn of attention,
and Coltrane came.

This was no everyday event:
reports of madness
with too much technique
for the life force,
the flow tuned in and broken apart.

Infections of the middle ear
gave you the inflection
you couldn't hear,
patterns given in pleurisy,
each breath killing your timing
until you drowned,
went to drugs,
the iron body
with strings
solo.

OBSCURITY

When he lost his leg
above the knee
he wasn't drunk;
cold sober
and sweet in the cheeks,
his compositions
on FM radio
right next to his mouthpiece,
woodshedding, leading the war.

Then there was the year of bad
phrasing; another, content,
with short interludes
of playing too loud.

Most women couldn't stand it;
not *his* woman,
who thought Lester Young
was an excuse
for Coleman Hawkins,
two family names
on the same instrument.

Disc jockeys were favorable
after the leg was gone;
blind with diabetes,
still drinking *rooster red,*
he could come alive
in jam sessions
with another's mouthpiece—
his own in the woodshed
housing the wooden leg.

"ENGAGEMENTS"

To work steady you play the easy
tempos; drinks, on the starched
tab, are free; a flask hidden
from the cleaning lady.

Engraved by a club owner,
short on grit and sentiment,
he went sweet and lost his teeth
while still in his teens;
the roll of the bhang,
on Arabian paper,
couldn't save him,
stocking cap pulled down
on each player's ears.

Alive, on the tab,
and no credit for his song,
he was forced to mingle in the crowd,
some of the best-dressed
losers in the world.

There was smack:
oh the distances you could make up
in a hurry
with the proper bloodstream,
payback,
the cost of the song.

Rage at the hottest tempos,
or play slow.

PRESTIGE

Label in a period,
electrode for a voice
only Tatum can afford to sing:
imagine Shearing trying to cut Bud,
even in blindness, and Bud,
unable to play anywhere—
everybody backing off his left hand,
his sitting upon it, the alcoves
full of amphitheaters
in his head.

"I could play organ,"
he would say on the train
going uptown—"like Fats,"
his adopted sisters
scrambling the Jesus ballads

the wisdom of knowing
he never said a mumbling word—

RUMORS

When Miles smacked your face
for playing the right notes;
after the encounter, your solos
paralyzed the audience.

Left-handed players had no heart;
religion was an end-stopped
melody, *the* broken chariot.

Players from Philly
afraid to come to New York—

your liberty bell splattered
on the *AME* congregation,
readers of music, composers
who wrote down the group-effort song.

Spirituals have nothing to do with the church choir;
you lived or died on your instrument,
you died or lived on your instrument.

SUGARLOAF

Up-tempo ruined his style;
Trane would come in,
ruining the fabric
of swing, of bebop.

At the bridge Chambers would stop
humming in the high registers,
Philly Joe in the outhouse
kicking his traps,
one last exit blocked for Garland,
out-of-doors in block chords,
trying to double-clutch and catch up,
giving the finger to the engineers.

We are always on our best audience,
resting on the breastbone
of each performance,
refusing, in greasepaint,
and monkey suits,
to entertain, the mask
on blonde fables at midnight,
without candlelight.

In Newport (Sweden was over)
there was only Japan,
the taste of Blue Note,
the only sheet music
you could read.

When you pay the heavy dues of practice
play through the pain;
the easy chops are for playing after the break,
nowhere to go but the ruined swoops
of the counterpuncher,
unwinding to cycles of Lester
leaping in waterfalls of addiction:
paychecks for the bills long past due.

PULP NOTES

Too small a boy to play up front
of the band, but learning,
"all the things you are," to be heard,
"now's the time," above the drums,
before that the tambourines,
the whole aisle of women
just behind the beat,
and me, opting for Brooklyn,
after the whole middle class
had split—my fingers,
had I been gifted for the keys,
would have had their bandages
in ivory,
the honed protection of melody—
all I had was strings.

Four-hour layover
in the sack with a gorgeous whistle,
the whole city of Detroit
blanketed with snow
and nobody mad,
not a soul on overtime,
the meters, measures of skin,
a booming business.

Though I hated clichés
I never learned to drive
like Peddiford,
his Indian face
the best reason only blacks
take pictures of blacks.

Smack took my wrists
but the blood wouldn't give up
until I developed cancer,
no musician's disease,
a string man raised on pigmeat
eating himself.

I dreamed myself
learning to play at my own
funeral, in dress pants,
pimping in the gallery,
leading the blind to the trough
where all could drink:
tinkering with homemade radios,
invited to concerts on campuses,
where I was learning to read,
enough good music to play
in the bodies of the women
I came to know in the ballads,
forgetting how to keep myself alive.

MY BOOK ON TRANE

Waiting in lineups
in the rain you hear cosmic
conversations, "how many feet
above sea level,"
as though you could sign up
to play with Trane in the back room.

"What's the point waiting
for the last set if you can't see,"
and you smiling, underage,
protected from the blonde waitresses,
your new wife chilled to the bone
adrift in the fog of this music.

Every fool thought Trane should be taller,
an oak standing in water in his alligator
shoes, nobody able to hear Jimmy above the deafening
timber of Elvin, always able to hear.

Sonny, "just out of retirement,"
traveling with barbells,
had to have somewhere to play;
Clifford's dead; Miles won't play
facing crowds, addicted to playing "live."
One night I thought I'd have to squash
my hero, a dime-sized table, him
with his cuffs in my drink, peering
into the blue-green waters of Hawaii,
off Broadway, the Black Hawk, in North Beach.

Aiisha's always prettier in the rain,
the music loudest outside
coming into the brake—
the smoke coming off Elvin
as he strides across the street
to a working phone,
just like jet lag:
you can't believe the arc of light
in plain sight:
waiting for the drum major
from Pontiac with his brothers,
the steam coming off his wet clothes
in droves.

for McCoy Tyner

Stutterer

Protea Station, Soweto

No matter where he looks
he jumps to his own breath,
semiconscious in Xhosa
semiliterate in Afrikaans
news, his remembrance
of English editorials
he is forced to read.

His bamboo baton
rolls across the interrogation
table as disclaimer
after sessions at midnight.

Three kinds of explosives
line the flowchart nailed
on the bulletin board,
one photo of a pair
of miner's boots
itemizes devices
in heel and sole.

You can't call the consulate
secretary, or order lunch,
the briefcase search
is routine, its broken slats
exposed as film
in towers of light
over 16 June Soweto
in quest of development.

Fingers separate in linkage
of starter and fix;
a high-contrast print
like a summer's
day in wintry Jo'burg
rises to the top of a teacup
and the major checks permits
for the Europeans as our escort
says "all Americans are non-
European in Soweto."

The Militance of a Photograph
in the Passbook of a Bantu under Detention

Peace is the active presence of Justice.

The wrinkles on the brown face
of the carrying case
conform to the buttocks,
on which the streaks of water
from a five-gallon can
dribble on the tailfront
of the borrowed shirt
he would wear if he could
drain the pus from his swaddling
bandages, striations of skin
tunneling into the photograph.

This is no simple mug shot
of a runaway boy in a training
film, Soweto's pummeled wire,
though the turrets of light
glisten in smoke, the soft
coal hooding his platform
entrance, dull and quiet.

His father's miner's shoes
stand in puddles of polish,
the black soot baked
into images of brittle torso,
an inferno of bullets laid
out in a letter bomb,
the frontispiece of one sergeant-
major blackening his mustache.

On the drive to Evaton
a blank pass away from Sharpeville
where the freehold morgans
were bought by a black bishop
from Ontario, Canada, on a trek
northward from the Cape in 1908,
I speak to myself as the woman
riding in the backseat talks
of this day, her husband's
death, twenty-three years ago,
run over by an Afrikaner in the wrong
passing lane; the passbook on the shoulder
of the road leading to Evaton
is not the one I have in my hand,
and the photograph is not of my great-
grandfather, who set sail for Philadelphia
in the war year of 1916.
He did not want a reception, his letters
embarking on a platform at Queenstown
where his eloquence struck two Zulu warriors
pledged to die in the homelands
because they could not spin their own gold.

These threaded heads weigh down the ears
in design of the warrior, Shaka,
indifferent to the ruthless offerings
over the dead bodies of his wives,
childless in the campaigns with the British,
who sit on the ships of the Indian Ocean
each kraal shuddering near the borders;

her lips turn in profile
to the dust rising over a road
where his house once stood;
one could think of the women
carrying firewood as an etching
in remembrance to the silence,
commencing at Sharpeville,
but this is Evaton, where he would come

from across the galleyship of spears
turning in his robes to a bookmark;
it is a good book, the picture of words
in the gloss of a photograph,
the burned image of the man who wears
this image on the tongue of a child,
who might hold my hand
as we walk in late afternoon
into the predestined sun.

The press of wrinkles on the blanketed
voice of the man who took the train
from Johannesburg
is flattened in Cape Town,
and the history of this book
is on a trestle where Gandhi
worshipped in Natal,
and the Zulu lullaby
I cannot sing in Bantu
is this song in the body
of a passbook
and the book passes
into a shirt
and the back that wears it.

A Narrative of the Life and Times
of John Coltrane: Played by Himself

Hamlet, North Carolina

I don't remember train whistles,
or corroding trestles of ice
seeping from the hangband,
vaulting northward in shining triplets,
but the feel of the reed on my tongue
haunts me even now, my incisors
pulled so the pain wouldn't lurk
on "Cousin Mary";

in High Point I stared
at the bus which took us to band
practice on Memorial Day;
I could hardly make out, in the mud,
placemarks, separations of skin
sketched in plates above the rear bumper.

Mama asked, "what's the difference
'tween North and South Carolina,"
a capella notes of our church choir
doping me into arpeggios,
into *sheets of sound* labeling me
into dissonance.

I never liked the photo taken with
Bird, Miles without sunglasses,
me in profile almost out of exposure:
these were my images of movement;
when I hear the sacred songs,
auras of my mother at the stove,
I play the blues:

what good does it do to complain:
one night I was playing with Bostic,
blacking out, coming alive only to melodies
where I could play my parts:
And then, on a train to Philly,
I sang "Naima" locking the door
without exit no matter what song
I sang; with remonstrations on the ceiling
of that same room I practiced in
on my back when too tired to stand,
I broke loose from crystalline habits
I thought would bring me that sound.

Driving the Big Chrysler
across the Country of My Birth

I would wait for the tunnels
to glide into overdrive,
the shanked curves glittering with
truck tires, the last four bars
of Clifford's solo on "'Round Midnight"
somehow embossed on my memo stand.

Coming up the hill from Harrisburg,
I heard Elvin's magical voice
on the tynes of a bus going to Lexington;
McCoy my *spiritual anchor*—
his tonics bristling in solemn
gyrations of the left hand.

At a bus terminal waiting to be taken
to the cemetery, I thought of Lester
Young's Chinese face on a Christmas
card mailed to my house in Queens: Prez!
I saw him cry in joy as the recordings
Bird memorized in Missouri breaks
floated on Bessie's floodless hill:
Backwater Blues; I could never play
such sweetness again: Lady said Prez
was the closest she ever got to real
escort, him worrying who was behind
him in arcades memorizing his tunes.

Driving into this Wyoming sunset,
rehearsing my perfect foursome,
ordering our lives on off-days,
it's reported I'd gone out like Bird

recovering at Camarillo,
in an off-stage concert in L.A.

I never hear playbacks of that chorus
of plaints, Dolphy's love-filled echoings,
perhaps my mother's hands
calling me to breakfast, the Heath
Brothers, in triplicate, asking me to stand
in; when Miles smacked me for being *smacked
out* on "Woodn't You," I thought how many
tunes I'd forgotten in my suspension
on the pentatonic scale; my solos
shortened, when I joined Monk he drilled
black keys into registers of pain, joy
rekindled in McCoy's solo of "The Promise."

What does Detroit have to give my music
as elk-miles distance into shoal-lights,
dashes at sunrise over Oakland:
Elvin from Pontiac, McCoy from Philly,
Chambers from Detroit waltzing his bass.
I can never write a bar of this music
in this life chanting toward paradise
in this sunship from Motown.

Peace on Earth

Tunes come to me at morning
prayer, after flax sunflower
seeds jammed in a coffee can;

when we went to Japan
I prayed at the shrine
for the war dead broken
at Nagasaki;

the tears on the lip of my soprano
glistened in the sun.

In interviews
I talked about my music's
voice of praise to our oneness,

them getting caught up in techniques
of the electronic school

lifting us into assault;

in live sessions, without an audience
I see faces on the flues of the piano,

cymbals driving me into ecstasies on my knees,

the demonic angel, Elvin,
answering my prayers on African drum,

on *Spiritual*

and on *Reverend King*

we chanted his words
on the mountain, where the golden chalice
came in our darkness.

I pursued the songless sound
of embouchures on Parisian thoroughfares,

the coins spilling across the arched
balustrade against my feet;

no high as intense as possessions
given up in practice

where the scales came to my fingers

without deliverance,
the light always coming at 4 A.M.

Syeeda's "Song Flute" charts
my playing for the ancestors;

how could I do otherwise,

passing so quickly in this galaxy

there is no time for being

to be paid in acknowledgment;
all praise to the phrase brought to me:
salaams of becoming:
A LOVE SUPREME:

From *Honorable Amendments*
1995

This is a penmanship
of song; we are journalists
for the race this Saturday,
in honor of Saturday's child,
a sacred seat with the father.

Intentional Suffering

The hat turned to match the trimmed mustache;
the basepaths you trod at Morehouse in white bucks;
the whole world on newsreel riding taxis called
"Free Ride to Heaven" and *Hate* Bus—
Kennedy, on new wheels, and partial to Hollywood,
comes to the rescue, with troops; recruits,
with upturned helmets, pray for early leave.

One horse, dead on arrival at Cottonwood,
is put to death again on the operating table,
the thrashing of his shattered stump
spraying the ceiling, smocks, doorhandles.
This is a horse that belongs to the mounted police.

The King of Sweden watched agog; on the elevator
in the old section of Stockholm *An America Dilemma*
becomes the practical light in the storm—
the scholars of the thirties put it down for good.

Eavesdropping by electrodes come to your door;
your children wake up and sleep quiet
to choir flashbacks to *Genesis,* the Golden Rule.
You finger the cotton robes given at gravesites;
you think of Sam Hose and Bennie Mays—
you promise anything to the country's conscience
in a hotel lobby, for cameras, for NPR.

Boston looks better the closer you get to the mountain-
top, which isn't Memphis or Birmingham, but Oslo,
when you were almost free from the FBI.

Ida, the housemaid from Augusta, Georgia,
walks to work on the day of your death
in a pink smock which she refuses to change.
Her son works at the arsenal; he moves furniture
for the good people of the military base
with an impish smile: his prayers are daily
prayers; on Sundays he gardens his own patch.

He remembers his mother's first impressions
of the good white people of the South,
with their lights on,
while the debate goes on for peace;
the family does not know his mother's surname.
He makes sure nothing shifts in the half-ton
that will scar or break on the turns
going by the military base. His text,
written in his mother's blood, is in capital letters.

To an Old Man Twiddlin' Thumbs

You sit twiddlin' thumbs
"beat out," watching
your wife watch you watch her:
all this watching twiddlin' thumbs.

My children fidget while you balance
thumb controls on local news,
excerpts from a recent book on slavery,
and we finally have the scale of twiddlin' thumbs.

Old man, remember the chemistry
for your depression is alchemical.
I set out my convivial tools
measuring your need, measuring your index
finger, your thumbnails, your wife
"beat out" in her slavery of affection
for your genius at disguise.

Old man, my pestle works for your recovery;
old man, the conjure knowledge is "beat out"
with alkaline and tea,
this nightmare where you've lost your way home:
old man, the strong men must come on.

Angola (Louisiana)

Three-fourths Mississippi
River, one-fourth rattlesnakes,
and for company, razorwire
fences, experiments from South
Africa, aging behind bars,
all in their seventies,
with no parole; perhaps
2,500 natural life sentences,
30-year lifers behind bars.

Still, the roads have flowers;
and in the prison hospital
the Lifers Association creed
is in full bloom, technical
supernovas of the TV world:
you avoid mirrors as you can't
avoid hard labor, false teeth,
high blood pressure, rape:
all this in the prison magazine.

Wheelchair has transcended mirrors;
he dreams about theft and harassment
as a prison underwater,
decompression channels of the bends,
cheap guards in scuba tanks,
for he is never coming up;
it is "too exotic," he says,
and you hunger for the fields
you were broken in;
you hunger for your white neighbors,
dragon deputies, the KKK,

as you count the gray hairs
on the sideview of your mustache.

After three heart attacks
you can stand gospel music,
sports, violence, drugs,
for deathrow education
is bimonthly books,
the old folks' home on this shuttle.

I was born on False River:
tell my story in amplitude
from one slavery to another;
give me the pure medicine
for rape, murder, the nectar
in balm for the barroom fight:
teach me to read, and write.

for Ernest J. Gaines

SONGLINES FROM A TESSERA(E) JOURNAL: ROMARE BEARDEN, 1912–88

"A style is achieved by an artist through his introduction of personal forms into the grand style of his period."

QUILTING BEE (MECKLENBURG COUNTY)

"Re PLUMMER ALEXANDER, born in August, 1853,
in North Carolina near Charlotte, near the porch
which he leapt from to travel north with Union
soldiers, Sherman's returning army, in 1865.
He was sitting on a fence, which was kin to the porch,
when troops passed by; one soldier offered to take
him north—Plummer never said good-bye.
              When he got to New York
worked his way to the stature of Huntington Harford's
valet; had been a "runner" on Wall Street; was taught to
read (as an adult) by his wife, Francis Moore, whom he met in Ithaca.*
What a resonant, mellifluous voice; returned home
to buy shoes for his mother; always reserved a Pullman
to avoid segregated travel. Loved trains; had trouble
with that mode of travel. Lived in East New York
into his eighties, walking miles to work in weather.
Any information you might find in state records
most appreciated."
              This over the bunting:
the diamonds and gold of musicians humming without voice.

*Underground railroad station (New York)

HOMAGE TO THE BROWN BOMBER

Speed of the punch,
its dancing, rhythmic fluency
in short space, short duration,
its honing light of the Garden,
the Stadium: each gladiator falls
to be redeemed in porcelain speech,
however simple, never glib,
the nation's devastation
coming home to roost.

Born near sacred Indian mounds in Alabama,
broken in the "destroy" kitchens
of Chevrolet and Cadillac,
short tours at Comiskey Park,
the heavy bag the strange fruit
of commerce, newsprint,
without the dazzling photographs
of Sonja Henie's pirouettes
at the Olympic games,
in shared bedrooms, horns
plenty for the unprotected.

Sugar dazzled too,
but the brute poetry
of the finisher,
how to wait on hidden impulse
of a bannered song,
that was ammunition
for the lost struggle
of the chaingang,
of the limousine.

Taps at Vegas,
new shrubbery
at Arlington,
grist for radio, the stooped flares
of camels
on deserts of yesterdays,
bright lungs blanching tomorrows,
barrows at rest.

JOURNEY THROUGH THE INTERIOR

"There is unfortunately no bridge between the fine arts and the arts of
commerce. The artist must decide which of the two endeavors is most
compatible to his talents and personality."

the unity is actual placement of stones
    its purpose: enhancement without disturbance

closure, its rests, grids, agitated surfaces
    bars of music, vertical control

I entered my canvas in Masonic calm,
    the open corner, with natural linen
    as all baptism is tearing upward
    astride flat surfaces
    with immaculate rice paper
scale is always the cut-out
    lost silhouettes:

    "it was like looking at pretty girls
and not being able to see beautiful women"

    It was strenuous repetition
    tempering of volumes
    as keys on Earl Hines's righteous
    black keys, its tensions
    overlapping the planes,
    the music of optics.

One avoids defeat when judgment comes slowly,
    mysterious as creation itself:
    structure often appears far apart
from images that animate dreams—
    no matter the effects they launch
are representational or decorative in nature.

    Nymphs at infinite depth,
    the bird is the fish the soldier the dancer:
    he who plays the inner music;
    she, the word, in aquarium.

ODD FACTS ABOUT THE PAINTER
(ON CAUSALITY)

"A realized structure is exacting in its spiritual and intellectual demands,
and it unites such complexities as a sense of the past, as well as the total
response of the painter to his craft, to himself, and to the life about him."

because robust sense of humor
     more subtle than tunes
     played in the head
     full of books, handkerchiefs,
     appurtenances at shared studios;
because conversations mean dance,
     vital steps for musicians
                    who walk on their horns,
     their reedy tongues praise-gossip
because Savoy had good stride-piano
     tusks of Arabian cloth/Hannibal's elephant nights
because we cut this crazy quilt for Aïda,
     paste up for Judith Jamison,
     sketch cranial wall of Negro
     History Week, crater cave drawings
     most subtle, opaque modern cube of subway;

because a few spatial conventions
     (Slavery, transatlantic triangular
     trade, econometric wood carvings,
     aesthetics of man, color combinations—
     mestizos/olé orishas—pictorial errors,
     miscegenated dross: the gene pool:)

because various problems of relationship
     condense negative space of temperament

why "Blue & Sentimental"
why "Jubilee Singers"
    why no bitterness in warm travels
    from Yoruba village to the block
    why block stays empty
    why roulette wheel to vespers
    why accented songbirds in large spaces
    why ecstasy, why agony
    because confidence is hand-papered
    paintings at joists, hoeing
    vertical connective tissue,
    circles of transition,
    children of Circé

because victory garden
    why report of munition
because unseen armature of soul
    why spirit faces in masks
    of breastbone, leg irons,
    leg bones, legba ginny
    because welfare avocation
    turns umbrella inside out
    because convex/concave tropes
    why primitive influence (man as art form)
    more expressive than technical
because nature worship means end of nature
    why Fang figure
    because meteors fallen on alien landscape
    (blacks in the south)
    why they belong there
    always cubicle projection:
    ritual love: the other monotheism: radius lens.

DEAR ROMIE: ROCK FORMATION EPISTLES

Thanks for the drawing of Judith Jamison.
Thanks for the color separation of six
Odysseus collages, a portion of the sequence
in ritual brightness; thanks for the suggestions
of Hannibal as a tactician; thanks for educating
William Carlos Williams about the pictorial phrase.
Thanks for having your own donated pictures framed
at your own expense at the Hilton Hotel (N.Y.C.)
for the Black Academy of Arts & Letters—
standing in line for the shrimp cocktail
was a ritual experience—one could hear the music
of Chick Webb and Lester Young at the Savoy
because you put it there in your rock formations,
contests better, at the level of art, than the Apollo,
no bad feat in bear markets. Thanks for all your visual
puns, blind alleys, pig Latin collage: what you said
about Picasso: "the artist's sense of space is something
at which he gradually arrives, and then usually keeps
intact the rest of his life." Thanks for making the calluses,
that knowledge that soaks through to your hands; thanks
for wanting to do so. Thanks for the opening:
how to get to the unseen, how to get off welfare,
roadmaps of the G.I. Bill, World War II,
discrimination, preaching, rent control,
rent parties, Masonic orders, April in Paris.
Thanks for first steps etched to radio,
your own imitations hidden in the dark;
thanks for the pictorial limp, in sacred territory,
of the gangs; thanks for the strawboss calling our names;
thanks for the secret society of a man and a woman
reclining, standing tall, shopping at the early market,

drinking at the late; thanks for the waltz of Ladies
Night, Blue Monday, "kitchen mechanics," the Harlem curfew,
the bouncers that control clubs, fair fights with ground rules;
thanks for the gang rules, marathons, jitterbug reputations;
thanks for not getting caught in "Movietone News"; thanks
for "having a ball doing whatever came into my head" through
those knowledgeable hands; thanks for reading Delacroix's journal;
thanks for listening to Claude McKay; thanks for not being thrown
by "air steps," thanks for your own brand of eavesdropping,
making it an architonic experience which speaks volumes;
thanks for that elite demographics, going downtown to museums
and uptown to museums, and, as Lester Young used to do:
"catch the rhythm of the dancers which always comes back to you
when you're playing." Thanks for your pace at the fair.

Portrait of James Weldon Johnson

Atlanta Archives

The rolled cigar: Nicaragua politics,
the jazz age sequestered 'round midnight;
NAACP business around the clock.

His novel a mystery,
certainly "autobiographical"
in the sense that he wrote it.

Carlo let loose on the Harlemites;
he flicks the switch of the publishers,
eats cognac, eats champagne,
his Iowan teeth like headlights
from Jay Gatsby's coupé.

Reading for the cigarmakers
is not laughter, and not to be laughed at;
good cigars are a novelty
to tourists, but for quality,
white and black, the best
leaf for the book,
smelt of print,
and away from the print,
stylized segregation.

Housing patterns are to be cashed in on;
Strivers Row are bungalows
compared to plantations;
for immigrants,
just off Ellis Island,
they are goldmines
and golden business.

From the Atlanta Archives
four coattailed *sports*
are about to go out on the road.

Hair parted, not a smoker
in the bunch, Weldon tunes up
his infield for the orchestra:

This is GA; it is a town
Du Bois walks in; commercial peachtree
is not the apple of his eye;
he remembers the Seminoles
above all Indians; railroads
are a checkered experience,
chaingangs, turpentine wards,
bring him the blues. He begins to read in Georgia.

The Caribbean calls to understand
revolution; Garvey gets to town
just in time; in Niagara, over the falls,
the braintrust works out strategy.
In eighty years we'll be ready to tackle
Latin America; *Plessy v. Ferguson*
is barely cold. The marshals of progress
turn their phases on stock prices;
the stock is paper or it's meat.

Archives

Cooperstown, N.Y.

Photos and clippings fade;
no one can find a real signature
of Rube Foster, who put together
the Negro Leagues; efforts
at why Josh Gibson died at thirty-
five are even vaguer,
his sleek strong body in the waves
of San Juan the vintage year:
1934. Later, 72 home runs,
the only ball over the third tier
at Yankee Stadium
for the games on off-days.

No flicks of Gibson as a Globe-
trotter, his golden gloves
astride the mound captured,
for real, with Curt Flood,
eating steaks on a grill,
in a parking lot in spring
training. Reggie is a mask,
astride a roadster, a paltry
lid on a rainday with Vida Blue.

Frank Robinson's loaded automatic
put him under arrest; the flick
of his headrag, a white mop,
only shown in Cincinnati,
eating Satchel's 45-lb. catfish,
chasing "Willmont" Liquors, Inc.
as endorsements in Brooklyn.

The clippings of the rest
of Negro America are full of glee;
no ounce of bitterness,
except for Jackie, who hit
better than they thought,
and was fast, stealing home
in public, voting Republican,
the whole Civil War
on his back and pigeon-toes.

On PBS the documentaries,
one trailer sideshow,
a whole hall of oral history
in transcriptions
of black and white.

Trujillo, who paid the best,
threatened execution if you lost;
the black World Series in Comiskey
full of chicken, zoot suits,
trainfare from everywhere
but endorsements, turnstyles.

"Let's play two."

The Ghost of Soul-Making

"On that day it was decreed who shall live and who shall die."
—Yom Kippur prayer

"Art in its ultimate always celebrates the victory."

The ghost appears in the dark of winter,
sometimes in the light of summer, in the light
of spring, confronts you behind the half-door
in the first shock of morning,
often after-hours, with bad memories to stunt
your day, whines in twilight, whines in the umbrella of trees.

He stands outside the locked doors, rain or shine;
he constructs the stuntwork of allegiances
in the form of students, in the form of the half-measure
of blankets—he comes to parade rest in the itch of frost
on the maple, on the cherry caught in the open field
of artillery; he remembers the battlefields of the democratic
order; he marks each accent through the gates of the orchard
singing in the cadences of books—
you remember books burned, a shattering of crystals,
prayers for now, and in the afterlife, Germany of the northern
lights of Kristallnacht, the ashes of synagogues.

The ghost turns to your mother as if he believed
in penance, in wages earned, in truth places these flowers
you have brought with your own hands,
irises certainly, and the dalmatian rose,
whose fragrance calms every hunger in religious feast or fast.
Into her hands, these blossoms, her fragrant palms.

There is no wedding ring in the life of ghosts,
no sacred asp on the wrist in imperial cool,
but there is a bowl on the reception table,
offerings of Swiss black licorice.
On good days the bowl would entice the dream
of husband, children, and grandchildren;
on good days one could build a synagogue in one's own city,
call it *city of testimony, conscious city of words.*
In this precinct male and female, the ghost commences, the ghost
disappears.

What of the lady in the half-door of the enlightenment:
tact, and a few scarves, a small indulgence for a frugal
woman; loyalty learned in the lost records of intricate relations:
how to remember, how to forget the priceless injuries
on a steno tablet, in the tenured cabinets of the files.
At birth, and before, the ghost taught understanding:
that no history is fully a record, for the food we will eat
is never sour on the tongue, lethal, or not, as a defenseless
scapegoat, the tongue turned over, as compost is turned over,
to sainthood which makes the palate sing. These are jewels
in the service of others; this is her song. She reaps
the great reward of praise, where answers do not answer,
when the self, unleashed from the delicate bottle,
wafts over the trees at sunrise and forgives the dusk.

for Ruth Oppenheim

Studs

Off-color eyes that shine through lobes,
the flesh still uneaten by stickpin,
he was stuck to her; this attachment,
like string from the loops of IUD
caught him unawares, in planes
above the Earth, on plains
near the homestead, on water
which he has touched with his belt
and bow, as a lifeguard,
before he met her.
                              Yes, she could brown
in that sun, the broad shoulders
concealed in flesh for his children,
who grew beyond her; he built a shed
for her tools, the garden, the chain saw—
windows faced toward the southern estuary
where turtles called, for the pond
swelled in the porous ground,
from springs, and she was a spring.

All day he has thought of Seminoles;
all day he has dreamed of the Narragansett;
his children could fit in if the drum
were opened to shells he could use
for the dinner table, and shells
from the sea decorate the walls
of the uterus, mystery of caves
he got lost in on special dates,
January 15 for instance,
now a national holiday;
and April 23, her father's birthday,
and Shakespeare's,

where he read in a long line
at the Library of Congress
after visiting the Capitol
where Martin Luther King Jr.
stood in consummate black stone.

Now he must ask about diamonds;
how refraction turns into bloodlines
he could choose for band music,
the territory bands
of Count Basie, without charts,
in a beat-up van,
passing for Indians,
passing in the slow lane
through the culture.

He would place her flesh there;
he would ask her to wear these,
diamond studs, in each ear,
to hear his song: to hear his name
come alive in her ears.

My Father's Face

Schomburg Archives

Over his fastidious hands
his voice breaks,
and because he had executed
the bequest
(typing the book lists
sermons in manuscript
& unlisted artifacts)
on his son's birthday
in the Brooklyn brownstone,
this is a double loss,
unbeknownst, even to him,
at this late date
in the March snow,
how much the past costs;
how much the health
of one's nation
as neighborhood,
is stored in the family,
the archives,
the handwriting
of our saints & sinners,
and the forgiveness
of sin's remembering.
(As for the saints)
For now the ancient folders
are enough for the sorrow,
which is grief over my mother's
life, and the grand thematics
of a little girl,
polishing her jacks

on her grandfather's marble
steps, too close, even for him,
to the Germantown governors
who account for the meal
and his till.

We are here on the edge
of another parade,
a huge mural
as a gate,
east and west,
in honor of Nat Cole's walk,
as if his majesty
on the keyboard,
the lilt of his Montgomery
voice,
was a memorial to running water,
to stone, and the masonry
of singing on the stone,
which was his pledge,
which was his right.

This is the penmanship
of song; we are journalists
for the race this Saturday,
in honor of Saturday's child,
a sacred seat with the father.

Thimble

My mother loved Philadelphia
because her grandfather
preached there;
"come on, Jack,"
he would say to her sister
when he made his rounds,
and not so often,
when he needed an "Amen,"
from that little girl,
bright as a thimble.

Henrietta, dressmaker-queen
of small sizes
must've known the Simon brothers,
the Welsh immigrants,
so she gave the touch
to my mother, who loved
Mexican silver.

In the glass dome,
your sterling notebook
tells the comprehensive
story as a memoir
of the underground railroad,
if anyone in this world
wanted the full story.

We are reduced to
"called to meals,"
and glad to get them
having graduated
from gruel to capons.

Still we can lay on
the silver, when we have to:

your newsladen epistles,
over fifty years,
make up the patchwork
of a nation's understory,
birds migrating
as friends,
from the other world.

    for Lois

Peace Gene

"A niger
is living proof
that Indians
fucked buffalo"

Irish Suit

He carries my Irish tweed
all the way from Strand Rd.
to suburban London;
in bicentenary exchange,
Ireland is skipped,
Yeats, father of us both,
in "responsibilities"
has the wrong politics.
　　(After Long Silence)
The man comes alive first,
in Berkeley, though his woman
was attacked there,
we read the divine lyrics
of chairman Walcott
near Philadelphia,
but little liberty,
in Atalanta,
your Ellmann lectures at Emory
So we did it again, read for cameras,
Polaroids, Jameson.

I save my suit for Iowa
when I had no clothes for winter;
at Oxford, in June, with no classes
in session, we sent out students
to the pubs, and had an audience:
1976 Soweto in Afrikaans news
in the *Irish Times* where you
wrote reviews, essays of the Left
and Right. And the Right moved left to
Chekov/Dante/Philoctetes

My kids got lost in Balleyvaughan
in the Irish kitchens 'til
the British came on holiday—
then, Irish figures, stock
characters of the joke,
took us to tragedy,
which is black Irish, blackbush,
black&tan, black&white
race/rituals of America,
each patriot playing his assigned
part; I name one son Cuchulain
and he fought the ungovernable
sea, as Auden did in 1939 on Fifty-second St.

Isherwood was my camera;
he brought Laughton
(hunchback of Notre Dame),
his next-door neighbor,
to class, without notice:
then came Auden, Spender, Huxley, Heard
but no Americans, and so my tongue
has gone black & blue, $^3/_5$ confection
of Milton while in jail on assault
protecting myself in a black neighborhood
from white transients: Lucifer
gets our best efforts,
but he wears this Irish suit,
to line his pants, homemade cloth of the wellhead.

April 13, 1939

Strands

Hold fast to conscience and push deliberately towards self-mastery.
—Seamus Heaney

Upstairs in the high perch
the strands of coal light
discoursing over the house
and cottage in County Wicklow
the burial ruins
temper the light of the skull
shone on our heathen forebears,
sunlight and periscoped
floss of Catherine's cries
in the glen where the turret
north of Belfast sited your kin.

Of course we shop at McDonald's
for nourishment, though the Easter 1916
room is closed to the staffers' lunching
over the great nags and knitters
of the earth and song.

In the post office I photograph
my three children in front of *Cuchulain*
tied up so he won't die on his back—
the mail goes out in regulations
and stamps among the bullet holes,
letter bombs, encasements
of stone and countryside.

I hear a voice around the devil's glen,
alms to the monastery with draw ladder,
bridge and waters glistening

with legionnaire coins: the pirate
monks, my children in the high
fields of automatic camera
and the writing.

With no central heating, and no poem
for Robert Lowell, crossing over
in the taxi in New York
I think of Wordsworth in his public
school, Hawkshead,
where my woman split her lip
dreaming of a pewter man
pruning my apple orchard
on ladder and rused thorn
in the eye as I left the country.

Ditties you would sing
of Charlie Chaplin, the Dardanelles
of coal stove and bath
in the intuitive showers where
memories are old identities—

Aborigines (Estonia)

"Language is the only homeland."
—Czeslaw Milosz

In a special audience,
with President Meri,
who has eight languages
under his many belts,
his secretaries in the cold
palace protected by guards
without bullets in their ancient
guns, and after exchange,
foreign and domestic,
I read a poem of welcome
to him, who could have gone
to graduate school in America,
but was sent to Siberia instead.

And I wait for the silence which is a bookman's
special pleading, and ask him where, on the map,
which is as ancient as his ancestors, where was that town
he was sent to:
              the globe rests on his writing table,
but he goes for his books, translated in several
languages, for a handwritten inscription
from his father, who was a scholar/writer
in his own write, and wrote poetry in Estonia,
a poetry unsaid in every privacy, since '17.

He points to the outpost, then, casting a glaze
across the Bering Sea, points to Alaska
and beyond: "the only thing that kept me alive
in that dreadful time was the thought of the aborigines"—

this could be Indians surely, the Inuit, who have no written
language, but sing their songs of acceptance
in tones so sweet even blubber, succulent
in the worst winters, answers back, as every spirit
of the world talks back in the song of the singer.

But he does not mean them; he means, it is clear,
for the time he takes to make his prepared entrance
to the map, he means writers, Americans,
who have taken his time from affairs,
and he welcomes this time away from disaster.

Only a little later, the whole world comes alive
in the estimates of hatch and water in the ferry
named for a free country: some nine hundred passengers
and crew went down and out and we sent messages
to President Meri about bad times, disastrous
times, and the nuanced poetry lost with these souls.

I photographed the *Estonia* from my hotel perch,
anchored in a hail of sunlight, a beam-ridden morning
that is not the character of the sea;
and when we visited Uswa, and stood before
Gustavus Adolphus, and thought of Jesus in the old
world, we knew the cadence of this song:
aborigines: beginners at the salt-lick
of citizenship, paid for in the extreme,
and free for the very asking,
frostdriven on a map in Siberia.

for President Meri
Estonia, September 1994

marginalia

"Nothing fixes a thing so intensely in
the memory as the wish to forget it."
—Montaigne

Planes overhead, snipers with their Tijuana
Bibles in their backpacks,
                          this isn't Windsor
Village, or your missing brother
in his narrow hallways of magazines (both kinds)
and books (all kinds)
                          and the war novels
of Coleridge, our native bibliographia/
honoraria, and Twain (not Montaigne)

and certainly not opera. The singer
is back in the tree; his looking glass
is the spiderweb of the cross hairs,
vectored membranes of radar:

the age has been full of commuters;
again we are at war.
                          I would build,
in your treehouse, a few odd jobs
for the victory garden, exotic plants,
Andromeda in the periphery of stunned museum glass,
and the centuries would go back and forth
across the equator.
                          Africa would be heard
again, as with the ancients,
and songs of science would be the poems of praise. Praise song.

Auden came once to my undergrad class,
Isherwood attending; I was asked to welcome
our guest with a public request; since this was
not Yeats at hand, I asked for recitation
of "September 1, 1939," and the man with the quaint
eyebrows of perpetual surprise nodded.
Auden talked in his own metrics, a memorized
misspent, perfect speech, for forty minutes,
all before 11 A.M.

On birthdays we are lost in the realm of the tall tale:
truth slides back and forth behind paintings and books
as the local lizards, which should not be killed.
Notes, as initials in braille, pile up on postcards
we are a little drunk on our own mileage,
but dearly lost and found on rites
and right-of-ways.
                    We are too near the airport
for a grand getaway; up north, snow and taxes,
laureates of the *Boston Globe.*

We are back to the brother of the book,
its many pages, revisions, the seams
our cut glass, those cross hairs:
our mission accomplished in the margins.

for Richard Wilbur,
on his seventieth birthday

An Umbrella of Maple Leaves

October 1994, Plainfield, Mass.

We park up off Lincoln St.;
men are working on the road,
we can plainly see,
right after the mailbox
marked "Ellison";
this is not a commodious
alley, or a gainly street,
but it has class,
its picturesque
turns, gulleys,
all of its pueblo-
like downhill,
is roughly elegant,
except in the season
of snowplow;
sometimes this road
is left completely alone.

Part of the barn is down
but that section up
is haunting, probably
because the grass
has been recently mown,
and further on, remnants
of garden, without fencing,
but clearly a sunspot:
all around the woods.

I remember a hammock
softly rocking between
trees, and Fanny,
unwilling to have her
picture taken,
with her arms around
her husband, who has on
a hat, no cigar, no pipe,
and from any position
when it comes to this girl
comfortable,
indulgent, his very own.

Now to the house, a cabin,
really, with an addition,
a study on stilts,
a huge desk, blue paper
of the tales of "Cleophus,"
hundred pounds too large,
and speaking to the author
over coffee, almost in the dark.
Cleophus always comes
to be heard.

The Writer's Desk

For a human being
who is an artist
the life is one
of twenty-four hours
and beneath the threshold
comes hence as a song
in deep sleep
be it day or night

You are a poet
all the time
(even when not writing)

and this equation
(two kinds of order,
geometric and living)
is Bergson's lost paper,
only one piece
over my whole life

the mystery to crack
is you (and so you rewrite
it): it wasn't good

over filtered coffee
in the early light
of Plainfield
I let Cleophus
visit amidst the maples
(On Lincoln Hill
he can come anytime;

300-kilo child
with a knack for trains
and the long whistles
through Arkansas
to Alabama)

I had a gun pulled on me
in Alabama
and went into the stacks
for William Dawson
and heard him speak
to the brick house of the wizard
and let the peanut go

in Dorothy Hall
I practiced when I slept
the veil over the fingers
on the face
was rising and falling

and the water cool as blood
which is why perfection
is possibility
the shadow in the act
on the gondolas

Paradise (Gihon River, Johnson, Vermont)

At Saratoga you were in whites
at the races, even the bucks
dancing a rhythm of money
if you were Scott Fitzgerald
but you were only on the make;
nothing short of an epic
would satisfy you,
and you were taking a day off
from the mansion at Yaddo;

I remember apparition
is what you most resembled,
and that R. V. Cassill
was a mentor
and you might be looking
for *Pretty Leslie*
or Profumo's girl
for subject matter;

you spent time here
according to the archivist
who wrote a history
of the college;
eighty-five with a bad heart
and seldom in his cups,
he mentioned when he retired
that he came back part-time,
and you are not recorded
in the history of the college,
which he had written;

he did mention you on campus
with a rifle—that if you taught
it was probably out of season,
and that you broke hearts
as the Egyptians did
in mummification;

the river is almost frozen;
I have asked for you;
the man who replaced you
edits the campus magazine
which is more than local;

there are painters and sculptors
passing through,
courtesy at the grand union,
French on local radio,
the border a half hour away;

Gihon is not in the dictionary;
you can hunt in the Bible
or gloss Milton
to find the tributaries
and transcendence;

they say you were drunk
as you went off the road nearby;
I hope you were:
Keats, who loved the word *azure,*
gave us the road map
for your condition:
bliss, ecstasy, bliss
as his letters say.

Pocahontas (Tuscaloosa, Alabama)

Shacks and palaces,
or the copies of them,
across this equatorial glade,

and at table, service,
me, a token of one,
you, a trustee,

and the touch of your fingers
on my shoulder
(when serving dessert)

is all the assurance
I need for caretaking,
and so I describe you:

priestess, yes, in your apparel,
and the bun, its deep feral design,
becoming for your age,

and stature,
regal, even on this plantation,
which is the pageantry of blood.

Smock, your uniform,
is handmade,
and like all tents

commodious
for the smoke
in elevation

to the sky,
for every hearth,
imaginary and real,

is bowel, campfire,
smoke signals,
if one can read the signs.

This is the faculty club
and I am a visitor
and what is literate

in the heat of September
is a salient calm
as in dynastic orders.

For this meal,
ceremonial to the corps
as my office

to the cadets
in the Confederacy,
is psychic bivouac

and your bisque
hand-chosen, and handmade:

one is always maneuvering
in the fields of Owens,
Louis in the alluvial shadows,

while on the surface,
as a bug to be eaten
on the Black Warrior River,

Wallace, and the "Bear,"
in litanies of fast food
as you leave the stadium.

Sled

If we were in Minnesota in winter
we would be negotiating the curves

in a four-wheel, rec vehicle,
snowmobile, or sled

and it would be a sled
rotten at the core, salt as window sail

and mud spattered as no school bus
on the rural antways of pickup and drop

no ice fishing hole large enough
for *snopes* and no *snopes* smart enough

to fish in the open water:
they cheat, men and women

half-stewed in cabin fever
living the heat of sled

a broken-down vehicle of inertia and need
not derisive, not pretty, sometimes reliable.

Rhythmic Arrangements (On Prosody)

I was forced to memorize and recite
in front of an atonal white hostess

made to do it again in itemized lists
on Iowa tests in critical argot complicit

with theatrical end rhymes adrift caesuras
worrying the line of nothing in the gut

but worried by the count in country
and out when Auden's "memorable speech"

came forward in soft-shoe slippers
librettos in tone deaf strife was no self

hidden in structures of spite
no sex could congress and no respite

from antics of song the pentameter
sometimey syllabics/accentuals

betraying the throttle and trestle
of the bridge, choral elements spared

in the wrestle of hesitant speech
so sprung rhythmaticals of geechy-timbred

voice you carried as a load from slavery
certainly as if Elizabethan antics

of cross keys in upper registers a drone
to find motherly lode commingles

on the vertical the increments implode
as horizontal keyboards of a scene

the metaphysics of the theorists
enjamb at exegesis

of human standards which reflect
alternatives to genuflection

I was an altar boy to blooming Joyce
the hymnal broken in makeshift storefronts

who brought the spirit low on high
"guess I'll give it one mo try"

in a moment's notice you compose
wrangling half notes magical phrasings

in a voice lost/found in subway grids
handmade librarians of the heart and ids

Letter of Athenaeum Couplets
in Memory of William Strickland

There are golden fish in the waters of the temple:
tablets, tabernacle, toll gate when the mummy speaks

and banks at the watersheds on Egyptian paper,
for Egyptians did not play in their sacred scrolls.

Strickland knew the watershed of the Delaware
Indians; perhaps he felt the broken treaties

at the Cumberland, at Nashville, on the Trail of Tears;
perhaps his theory of the column was no Liberty Bell.

There was the theory of the temple in windowless light,
and of the mine at play in the face of the child;

the child read into the night with a bright lamp
of travel; fans of displacement, hostages, civil strife

were written down in the honest materials
of the Confederacy, and of the Union, as Lincoln said—

"The prayers of both could not be answered—
that of neither has been answered fully."

Out of discord and the epistyle of his own nexus of rivers,
out of surveyor's level came the ghostwritten parthenon.

His embers flag and heel on short supplies,
at the breaking point of a new bank building.

It is a city-state of antebellum ease,
morose isosceles triangle in the nation's trade:

How one stands on fallen arches of the national railroad;
how one talks at the singed lines of embarkation, of design.

The fish are Masonic orders with their hidden rituals of order;
they are mutant joys of ornament, battle stations of space and song.

Day Room: St. Elizabeths Hospital

Back on medication
he takes inventory
of the atmosphere:
up Cedar Hill
(not so far up
as Frederick Douglass)
he thinks of Booker
Taliaferro Washington
as the only literate
person in his hometown,
so close to being lynched
that even train windows
are framed portraits
for the scaffold;

"they want to bury
the hatchet,
and it's always
in my head,"

and we know
this is the gourmets,
Senegambians/
negritos
working for Treasury
or Union Station,
Harrisons,
after hours
Howard station,
along the long walk
"nommo dudu"

for it is over
as in Greenville
on the levee
with Bessie Smith,
who was very late
in the Smith family
of songsters;

warts and all
is what is asked for
and it is given:

"so you have heard of me?"
we have done this scansion
on your sacred
family of poems:
"every damned one of 'em;
I don't play favorites
with my chillen";

when I'm right
in the head
Rose Ann stands
behind me
in her bare feet
like Coolwell;
"When did you meet
her, Prof?"

"She was strolling
with niece and nephew,
one in each hand,
and when I saw her
I doublefaulted."

I asked her to put
her slippers
underneath my bed,
and she finally did

on honeymoon
in Coolwell;
the Bibbys
were my welcome table;

do you know
"Sister Lou?"

Prof, was it
Gunnar Myrdal
taking notes
in "Count Us In?"

honey, you must
be a student
at Brown;

isn't that the slave-
owning family
you studied in;

do you know
"Strong Men?"

How 'bout
"strong women";

I know "Ma Rainey!"
Bless you, honey;

"you must know
how the teachers talk;
I can make out
what you say"

"Uncle Joe,"
I replied;
is he cousin
to Joe Meek?

"like Topsy
they just grew"

I love the sun
in this room,
"cold, cold, hot, hot"

Messages as Translation

"Justice Shallow, I owe you a thousand pounds."
—Shakespeare

With all of Sterling's poems in Spanish
the committee waits for defense;
you cannot go before them
with your hands empty
so go before them full
of the saga of St. Elizabeths
when a chaplain went into his room

and introduced herself as a student of Housman
asking him to sign her book
she had studied as a freshwoman
at Brown University; was he that Brown?

The *Asiento,* the church's covenant
with the mercenaries to imprison
the tribes of the New World,
all that the *Alhambra* failed to do:
1492: to raise up the barbarians
into the aesthetics of design,
the garden of the self
in the glaze and patina
of black men and women

who could build the *Taj Mahal*
with their own version of bricks:
Douglass Hall, Sterling Nelson Brown
Hall, Arthur Paul Davis Hall,
Daisy Turnbull Brown Hall:
the planet marble; the planet Styx.

Falstaff, your *pass* protection is the arc
of St. Michael's "straight, no chaser" sword;
crooked is the speech of the inquisitors,
for they must have their music.

The Slim Greer of the elements,
all the forces of humor and travail
on the open road, is now in Douglass
Hall, and in the Founder's Library,
as in the study of the glass books;
there is no postal box on Fort Totten;
Kearny Street is still the *poet laureate's* house:

even in Spanish *Cervantes* holds the Inquisition
at bay (the Spanish Armada, 1588), defeats in *terza rima,*
so that each child would understand it,
women applaud it, men remember it:

so present *Southern Road* as your hymnal
on the long walk to the presidents of Howard;
"there's no hiding place down here."

Calligraphy

collaboration: we translated Senghor
                                  together
                         "Two Flutes"
                         I chose 'mayflies'
                                  dancing
                         You chewed French patois
                                  poaching butterflies

french pottery: in the countryside
                         Grey Poupon
                         dill hillside
                         du jour
                         Armagnac
                         sublime
                         in chitterling
                         casserole

didier: legalistic mind
                         illegal tender
                         Miami waves
                         spaldeen gums

                         turkish cigarillos
                         escargot
                         cataract soup
                         Tigris/Euphrates
                         nothing for Tigre
                         in the Nile

church music: mutant tambourine
                         man in tweed
                         kerchief a la coattails

village panache
astride limousine
streetcar;
       potent
mother fix—
       father synod
sisters sonata canebrake
in the arboretum
of hometown;
John Wesley's hymns
Brown's baptist slave trade

Hayden's fingering
classic bow tie

carnivore lifestyles
just below
the Seine
where you washed
your collars
borrowed Mona Lisa

rollicked in Algerian
cutback cuisine

folk belles lettres: your favorite Coolwell
"Sister Lou"
drove garden truck
through nursery
of design; evil
prosody
when you consider
life force pattern
of the soul
after Goree

Trane's "Spiritual"

come stomp with Dick
in Michel's attic:

longhand chapters
bearing doctoral feathers

your mother's plumage
reshuffled, sanctified

at the cemetery: down from Dunbar
up from Wright
chortled mayfly
'round midnight

in memory of Melvin Dixon

Sorbet

Morsel or ton exquisite, the power
of taste in sonics, the power of theme
endurance, the well you go to for thirst.

I wore my basque beret
in duplicate
in your honor:

standing in Atlanta
in a squad
I was asked by a Guadalupan
just back from the Sorbonne
"how much basque blood
I had";
host of Tuskegeeans
backed off the microphone
as if the wizard
were approaching
with a cane
(maybe the one used on him
in New York City);

no vestryman
from St. Phillips
could approach the dais;
uptown and downtown
leaps of song synapsed

and in Chicago
nothing is trivialized:

you get down
for a pedestal at cape
and up
into the choir
of allegiance:

this woman has carried mail
on every bad day for good;
she is our project;
for this june bug
open your screens
and bring your spoons:

elixir, essence,
all that you can take away

(bring some to get some)
homemade is the best

Double Sorbet

This is sherbet but it is Du Boisian
with flavoring so sorrowful shenanigans

shake to meltdown and we are eating again.
The palate of observation exquisite

ever-presently in a prosody of lace
embroidery strengthened in homespun

patterns of speech the skipping rope
in alleyways compost on thoroughfares

commence symphonic tones of yesteryear
odors from the kitchen balm for hungers

only slightly felt in the name of bbq
sauce homemade the vinegar and salt

equations you can never solve without touch
do not eat "hold on" sorbet in G.B.'s name

a perfect temperature woven in the corner
of the Frigidaire too many morsels to eat

at one sitting the doubling overdraft
in the bank deposits one cannot save

but remembers in tintypes only she has made
an album still crisp with bacchanalia

refrains of living on the edge of train tracks
north and south of the equator

she navigates in some nightrain discourse
with the other cautionary tales

only sage can know and being 81
a tune Miles Davis played on Calumet

she is the traveler as archetypal jaguar
convivial enough as embers reach dusk

comfortable in the tree line off the ground
eating a catch mysterious and polish off

by double sorbet essences of fruit fructose
too sweet to be eaten before the meal: and saved

for edification in the logos of the race
above the veil, inside it, dawn to dusk

Triple Sorbet

Not Nero's flavor
when he ordered his runners

to bring fresh snow
topped with fruit juice and wine

not Catherine de Medici's
wedding-alliance with Henry II

her new sorbetto a rival
to literature and jewels

this is without sugar
the purees evangelical

with no concentrates
that are not molasses-black

both churn and still-freezing
without letting texture go

churn requires ice-cream maker
prepared a day early and allowed to breathe

still-freezing is a handmade technique
ice-cube trays covered with foil

all will last a month
if lumpy add Brazil nuts

too grainy cover with cream
underripe spike with gin or liqueur

I have seen soy and rice milk
fresh berries   granola

but senagambians and negritos
agree on mango   sometimes with rice syrup

cityslickers use ripe bananas
folks from the country   plantains

for the poet laureate of Illinois
fruit-of-the-Vine Elegant Gwen scoops

Wizardry: The Poetic Saga
in Song of Gwendolyn Brooks

When you wrote YOU WERE MY CLEAR WINNER
a telegram followed, wanting to publish,
but I held out for the critical word
from your typewriter; only later,
after my citation as honorand,
when Judge Sirica reigned
over Watergate, but did not jail
the real culprits—only then
did I appreciate, internalize,
conjure the special meaning
of your bold HOLD ON!

What you had learned in Topeka,
the rhythmic ropesters
dancing the neighborhood beat,
and how the count went up
IN THE MECCA, at vespers
in the baptist rectory,
which could have been a library
but had to feed the children
rereading their stories
you wrote for them.

We are lying about the sixties—
promise of any age—
when liberation is not Tupelo,
Natchez, including the trace,
and Hattiesburg
where women of grate song
and elbow grease
sat down through the floorboards
and gave their children up

into cold-water flats
and the ash and beeswax
of the Forty-seventh St. Y.

On the Brooklyn College campus
I spoke about the South African
connection with my ancestors
who bought the freehold land
before the Union became the Union,
and why the AME bishopry
had its gangster bishops
who sang their own religion,
with or without the spirit
which always rose to buzzard's
roost, to the rafters,
and on the choir's bench
satin dolls, and the rollaways
of our deep song,
louder than Bessie Smith's
"my house fell down and I can't live
there no mo"

And IN THE MECCA we could,
and in that narrative, sorrow songs
for the marathon of your committal.
The prizes in our hands were your words:

The Poet's Voice

"love, light, loss, liberty, lunacy
and laceration"
—Gwendolyn Brooks

Too much made of birth in Topeka
too little made of *Chicago Defender*

contributor at sixteen, the odd job
solo moments of community gloss

in each kitchenette clipping
microscopic tintypes of losses and gains

without the slightest naivete
of the street, backyard, parlor grid

her masterpiece of the "singing tree"
"We Real Cool" in 1959

anticipates the rest of the century;
after Fisk in 1967

known by detractors and sycophants
alike as "Mother Afrika"

but she remains a citizen in daily
interiors of unassailable synapse

contralto arpeggios released
in bemused attributes of light

at the end of her Lincoln West Tunnel
wordsmith of the "real thing"

exhortingly brave in every territory
for those unsung in service evermore

Reading from Isherwood's Letter Circa 1959–63

March 21. Saw Dr. Lichtenstein again yesterday evening. He assures me that my scar is healing normally. Many small nerves are cut through when the flesh is cut, and these are bound to hurt for a while. So I should just ignore the whole thing—and I will try to.

Last night we went to a goodbye party for Terence Rattigan, given by Hecht-Hill-Lancaster—more specifically by Hill, who is having an affair with Rita Hayworth. Because of this affair, apparently, Hayworth has been forced on to poor Terry as one of the stars in the movie version of his *Separate Tables.* She is somewhat spectral, now, but still, in a grim way, beautiful. Judy Garland looked like a cook, in a small white glittering round pie-shaped hat and a black dress that didn't fasten behind, because she's so fat, and that looked as if it might have come from the Goodwill. Lenore Cotten talked and talked and the two coons from Trinidad sang, while one of them scraped a gourd with a nail until all but the strongest nerves were ready to snap. Cedric Hardwicke's young wife insisted on sharing my chair, as she told me that Hardwicke was the kindest of husbands but that she has more fun when he's away.
—March 1957, *Christopher Isherwood Diaries*

In a crammed postcard, during the bicentary
exchange with Britain, I sent you word

of yourself, around 1936, as a memento to your goodly
instruction, in what could not be taught:

the landscape of the Brontës' moors, Sussex as an outpost,
"the White House" in elegant London

as a whorehouse, for the Arab oil moguls
(T. E. Lawrence on his motorbike over country lanes)

a reading list of mostly friends whom you brought to class:
Huxley, Auden, Spender, Heard, Laughton, Lancaster

as a platoon to vestrypacificism
encampment on Adelaide Drive

the impish vestigial laugh and pain in the gut
you disguised most ably when in company with Wystan

private vanities on the subject of Korea and Vietnam
the test of infantry hymns and foxholes between the wars

in Germany: penny loafers and woolen tie with work shirt
as a costume of the writer who has not written

lunches in the canteens of 20th, MGM, Warner Brothers
and the spread of forbidden fruit at Trader Vic's

Fred Shroyer's TV novel class with you as guest of honor
one-act plays in which the agents were musicians

who grew up on the Watts local, worked at Terminal Annex,
discussed Chopin and Debussy on the graveyard shift

of air mail, special delivery, and helicopter to LAX
the swimming pool in which the blackbird lifeguard chastens the
    metronome-

count in laps of the LAAC corpus of the Olympic team,
varsity across the street from USC and Exposition Park

and learning to serve at some distance as Pancho Gonzalez
gave "free lessons" to the "colored" kids at Rancho Park

next door to the Coliseum: All City Track Meet the race rituals of the
    Department of
Recreation and Parks telling jokes about "coons"

falling off diving boards, onto concrete, and not breaking
their skulls, and not learning to butterfly either

the Renaissance Club on Sunset Boulevard, where Dexter Gordon,
just out of Chino, came in to play the Sunday matinee

"with his ax and porkpie hat" in imitation of the president, Lester Young:
Dexter Gordon in the joint because of a stash of marijuana

which he inhaled; years of inhalation from Anniston, Alabama, army
   barracks
until Lady Day saved him from race riots with her song.

When you deliver newspapers in the white section of Baldwin Hills,
the *LA Times* becomes the paper of editorial delight

subscribers would meet your speeding car, downhill,
to pluck the ads and headlines from beneath the sprinklers

which were sprocketing their veiled spray over the grass,
rhododendrons, jacaranda, geraniums, Japanese gardeners

and at the end of the paper route, the sunrise, at the reservoir
and some fixation on the sprawl of L.A. going west, to the ocean

when, on bright days, you could see Catalina:
no paper allowed to be wet from grass or sprinkle

no actresses allowed to talk with Rochester
who kept Jack Benny in stitches, whose son,

Billy Anderson, made the '48 Olympic team as a hurdler,
who played defensive back for the Chicago Bears,

who ran the high school hurdles at Dorsey High School
in combat boots; who could broad jump from a standing

position over twenty feet, who high jumped backwards,
who was a terrible student made eligible by his grace alone

remember Howard Rumsey's All Stars in Hermosa Beach
the Pasadena Playhouse, reading at Huntington garden archives

Swerdlow's O'Neill seminar, "Epic of Search" class,
his lending his signed copy of *Invisible Man,* a tour at Dillard

how he was in the draft line, with Richard Wright,
in my hometown, Brooklyn; Calamus Club in *Invisible Man*

how James Baldwin wrote *Giovanni's Room,* on Bessie Smith records
"artists are here to disturb the peace" he said

introducing Malcolm X to the congregation on Central Avenue
the sickness of the West Side, for negroes, was gerrymandering,

the Santa Monica Freeway, and the Watts Riot
which I predicted lifeguarding at Willowbrook, in Compton,

at South Park, the Watts Poetry Workshop, Bud Shulberg's
contribution, *not making Sammy run anywhere*

but to early publication and sacrifice
to the media; remember Faulkner's admonition about *Soldier's Pay*

while "on the dole" writing scripts, and your hatred
of the tab you were on keeping you from your own novels, vedanta

and *solemn meditation*   with the elements   in the last search
unknowable essence of the Swami P.

You taught me the fables of William Golding on loan (in England),
refuted Philip Roth's accusation about voyeurism,

loaned me Arnold Wesker's plays, fought over *possum*
in Coulette's *War of the Secret Agents,*

fought Aristotle ("some men are natural-born slaves")
when black Alcibiades raised by Gilgamesh and Enkedu

after gang fighting in Peloponnesian wars
white betrayal (all God's chillun got wings)

black assassination (the Emperor Jones)
the intellect betrayed in Milton's *Paradise Lost*

in Pico Police Station cellmate thirty-third degree Mason
the career of the book now prison

to rescue the father as continuous bail
without the prism of *Black Orpheus* (the film)

the first act of liberation
is to destroy one's cage—

(Benito Cereno) (*My Bondage and My Freedom*)
in jail, out of jail, or no damn jail at all.

"Sinatra" (1915–98)

My father, born in the same year,
went to his own handmade cassette tape

when he heard the news: Cedars
never got over Ava Gardner

Maggio a hit because of Clift
the twin shadows of Hawaiian shirts

in the bombing of animal tension
song of the saloon of Jack Daniels

and mean even in the color scheme
of Las Vegas until he held the line

against segregation, Hoboken calm;
Palm Springs has a water fountain

in the waterline of Pal Joey
candidate Manchurian as he switched

allegiance in a dark suit Palladium
as the sox of Paramount took orders

took places where Riddle Basie were Capitol
in labels supreme as you drift into bites

of irony, afterglow, a scant frame
at the edge of conquistadorial defeat

c-notes of understanding
of how to win when up against the wall, always

Peace Plan: Meditation on the Nine Stages of "Peacemaking" as a Tribute to Senator *Claiborne Pell:* January 9, 1997

[define problem; you and me against the problem; shared concerns vs.
what you don't share; work on what is doable; work on listening skills;
have a peace plan; work on forgiveness; purify your heart.]

The *Trident,* in nightmare,
sits on the ocean floor;
the canopy of education
(as an active verb)
is sometimes schizophrenic;
its lessons lost in reflex
of the congressional record,
behind the iron and rice curtains
you wonder
what language the French spoke
in pronouncing Dien Bien Phu,
what part of our menu
still Hungarian goulash,
on what government menu
Kiev appears, or Riga,
or the Asian side of the Bosphorus;

a Pell poem should have a panel
in the civic square;
it should hold a pelican
who dines, always alone,
in the cemetery pyres
of the Revolutionary War Black Regiment
which is near his neighborhood;

it might strive, in perfect diction,
for clarity on the issues of sport;
at every hospital dance and shuffling

move to the whistles of the territory
bands; it is didactic in its rhythms
and it tells the truth;

I have sat in the waters of Foggy
Bottom, tape recorder going,
adjudicating individual grants,
and seen a henchman in the changeover
enjoy the joblessness of secretaries
who have worked freely on overtime;

I have appeared to the public
late Saturdays
slightly afraid of the punster
who has marked our regional
comings and goings
in the transfer of op-ed
and logarithm
and seen this calculus
reduced to novel synod
or tabernacle
or personal jurisdiction;

I have seen your principle
in the gait and habit
or staff, gallery, protocol:

it is a difficult peace plan:
prayer/service/nonviolence.

You are strong in the broken places;
we *could* win a war or an earthquake
if we embraced, in close quarters,
to ethical teachings the only answer
to a violent culture
(in *Trident*, in nightmare)

might protect even the aquifers,
conifers; our seas are idea rich
as plankton; as honest as pantomime

and we will find the intuitive organ—
the heart—and find the peace organ

and not let the year 2000
be compass alone
but compassion;
and know victims
understand violence best

and cultivate the peace gene:
the conflict resolution by example
of Claiborne Pell.

Notes on Making: The Heroic Pattern Updated: 1997

PROEM

The Hero's mother is a royal virgin;

His father is a king, and

Often a near relative of his mother, but

The circumstances of his conception are unusual, and

He is also reputed to be the son of a god.

At birth an attempt is made, usually by his father or his maternal grandfather, to kill him, but

He is spirited away, and

Reared by foster parents in a far country.

We are told nothing of his childhood, but

On reaching manhood he returns or goes to his future kingdom.

After a victory over the king and/or a giant, dragon, or wild beast,

He marries a princess, often the daughter of his predecessor, and

Becomes king.

For a time he reigns uneventfully, and

Prescribes laws, but

Later he loses favor with the gods, and/or his subjects, and

Is driven from the throne and city, after which

He meets with a mysterious death,

Often at the top of a hill.

His children, if any, do not succeed him.

His body is not buried, but nevertheless

He has one or more holy sepulchers.

1. Nevertheless it is a handicap only in time
   to be born "In the Mecca," or near it;

2. Fences are opportunities; family portraits
   are *sui generis:* that is, images to build on;

3. Dunbar's greatest gift was his psychograph;
   the smelt of logic in the elevator in Dayton,
   Ohio, got him to the world's fair (on borrowed
   time), however what is vocational tutelage?

4. Gladiators come to terms with self on the field
   of battle; this is interior discourse; there will be
   a wound (and a bow);

5. Arkansas Travelers are, by definition, mediators;
   the tribal sentience of flowers begins in torpor;
   oh chant of saints deliver me in vernacular chorus

6. I love the Quad Cities; one drafts as an animal
   drafts in the rows with a twin, Gilgamesh, Leadbelly,
   a guitar with no strings or those attached

7. rotisseries are the cylinders of invention; one stands on
   the confluence of rivers as latitude

8. defense is a tactical fence on the beer can highway;
   it is the place where vernacular becomes skyline

9. Ole! Prime numbers of heroes born on this date beware;
   what is the cosmic Ouija of destruction

10. to rejuggle the seeds of the periodic table
    in the forest, where one properly rests oneself

11. St. Louis is one station on the cross; beware of rivers
    no lithography can capture the color schemata, the valences

12. "Strange Fruit" as an elevator shaft; all labyrinths
    are museums without walls; the Illinois, difficult
    to cultivate the idiom of these indigenes; need implants

13. pictorial phrases, on any river, near Harriet Beecher
    Stowe porch, at the Taft, where Huck descends
    where Jim can be a man; wrong novel? vernacular regionalism

14. There are black lies in Newport, and sails in Virginia
    episodes of first colonies, riggings, Monticello artisans
    who stand as tall as the Black Regiment; in the same graveyards

15. One hits one's stride in Italy; marble, a medium to be
    ascertained in the quarry; you must teach your craft

16. which is touch; and the walls come tumbling down;
    cubicles are tight corners for new compositions a la Monk

17. Congo Square has always been part of Latin America;
    you must follow the sacred mounds from Arkansas
    longitudinally speaking

18. even Oprah has to learn to spell; out of great
    violation comes harmony: work in the broken places

19. for the strength of mother; it was the spirituals
the inmates from the death camps could sing; to their
golden parachutes Tuskegee airmen

20. 1492 the Moors driven out of Spain (and the Jews);
what is open for exploration is an increment of
revelation, even from the Vedas

21. there are equivalencies to sacred geometry;
you can hear this music deep in the compost

22. traverse where none can follow; love the self
first so all are purified by your example

～

Oedipus was not first, but swollen foot (to the Romantics)
meant "he who walks with pain"; (consider the source)

Theseus, grave unknown, but bones, supposedly, holy, in Athens;

Romulus, consult "Chariots of Fire" (not the movie; mother
trouble, glorious; how many lucky hills in Rome, in San Fran);

Heracles, his bow is needed by Odysseus; without that,
no resolution;

Perseus, watch Proteus; first dragon, as a man; few records
of succession, but, shrines everywhere;

Jason, golden fleece unexplored in this era; not shower of gold
on Perseus' shoulders, more shrine worship;

Bellerophon, attempted ascent to the sky, worshipped at Corinth;

Dionysus, Asia, laws in the grainery, visits the dead and talks
about it, ascends to Olympus;

Apollo, escapes by wile of his mother; no childhood but extant
at Delphi, kills python (long before Freud);

Zeus, marries his sister, hilltops particularly sacred to him,
muses (all nine of them), many edited Old Testament riffs;

Joseph, remember "Mandrake, the Magician"? good at dreams, fell
into disfavor even in Egypt;

(no need for Moses: however, Elijah victor at rain-making, plotted
against, and disappears in a chariot of fire).

Every artist has only a brief time for location,
to place himself (herself) between the tropics,
or outside them; making, the mode of creation,
is time-driven, and time-lost; it is the prime
mode; the elements are his/her vocabulary; yours
is only, on the very surface, biographical, but it
beckons promise of great resonance: 2000 is not
an accidental occurrence; Berlin is not only Hegel
and Beethoven; this timeframe is in heavy need
of translation; making is the key, not referencing;
but you are in a long line of cosmic makers; it is
in these unheard worlds you reign supreme; hence,
the opportunity: that is the making without predig-
estible category: it is the period of Joseph; let us
merit the modalities.

Mr. P.C., 1942–98, Bard College

I am angry with your passing;
so much to talk about Toronto

my relatives lost in transition
emigres to the States

the maneuvers they lived through
in itineracy on the missionary circuit

you were that: on a mission
I wanted to thank you for your touch

I intuited this, your touch
at the keyboard, in churches

on the river, at bay;
you took my boy on maneuvers

early and often, and then again;
now he is a man

with my druidic voice
whose timbre resembles arpeggios

I cannot play for you
I will stand at your gravesite

come summer, and think of "memorable
speech" as an Auden eclogue

to your memory, and remember my own
true marketplace, on the veld

which is your Hudson Valley
and my father's birthplace, in Catskill.

This was before the bridge;
his father cut ice in winter

and would not let my father clean toilets
which he cleaned himself

I could see you doing it
as the penultimate act

of a concerto
the music my son is writing

in your honor:
hear it in your wondrous sleep

old heart
for what you were doing among us.

Achebe at the Bridge

In the graveyards of the ancestors
Okike speaks; three decades
after the Biafran War a gate
to the golden stool, sacred
to the Akan, stands in the road

to the airport, and the flight away.
Vonnegut and Styron,
Fiedler, Bourjaily
campaign for the funds
to resist our policies,
and Fiedler says he will call
his old college roommate,
Henry, and get the facts:

we are in no hurry in the car
—the flight is late, and
silence fills the killing fields
in the tensions of grace,
for this is the true story:

and the word came back:
"this is not in our sphere
of influence"; "and I knew,"
you said, "millions of my people
would die."

This is no Ibo country,
not the province of the UN;
Kissinger, who is template
of the revenues of power
even now, is nobody's roommate.

And yet naiveté prevails
in the heart of darkness,
which is the heart of light;

we cross over as Horatio
crosses the Taghkanic;
the shield of Achilles is small;
logos in the West is just a story,
sometimes true;
yet the shadowbrother
manacles the stool to the father,
and mother stencils the sacred porridge
into a meal:

feeding the dead
is the only nourishment
for even the dynasties
of Nigeria

and you can go home
by air land or sea.

Faulkner's Centennial Poem: September 25, 1997

To MAMMY
(1840–1940)
Who was born to slavery and who
gave my family a fidelity without
stint or calculation of recompense
and to my childhood an immeasur-
        able devotion and love

This is the woman of *Go Down Moses,*
Caroline Barr, Mammy Callie,
suckler of your brothers and Jill;
you remember this tombstone
in the segregated cemetery,
the edge of the black section
buffer-zone to white Confederates
on campus and off:
                                Ole Miss
at Gettysburg is Ole Miss
at Oxford, and we are at odds
in the canebrake; this means

who is human and who is not;
the word *suckle* is in "The Bear,"

and in the quarters, it is the shack
where Mammy Callie lived;
it is the photograph a host took of me
from Memphis; it is miscegenation;
it is taboo; your heroes have gone
to New Orleans in guise of octoroons
and done the vestigial mathematics
of the gene pool; and come away
cleansed in the blood of the indigenes

who knew this story first
and left the spirit of place

in our idioms; the blacks took up
crossroad keys and amulets

and watered the fields
and planted up to the railings
which are always falling down.

You were a good postmaster;
we would like Mammy Callie on a stamp;
recompense is retribution:
"my house fell down and I can't live there no mo"
is what Bessie Smith sang
about that flood; the graves
of Ole Miss cannot be empty
in this empty-bed blues.

John Hope Franklin

The orchid your banner
its private fragrance white/black

1921 Greenwood aflame in kerosene;
not even *this* indentured

the wizard on maneuvers
on chair car and off

invitations up north
a tidy French cuisine

Toqueville's Auburn prison
not even approaching Harriet's

visionary quorum
Douglass alive at 54th sanctions

Saint-Gaudens curlicues
the national briar patch

concerto of Uncle Remus
Plessy v. Ferguson all business

even Thurgood's dirty jokes
made *gourmets* on commission

Brooklyn Bridge a high-water mark
for straddlin' fences

we are mending Tulsa's magnet school
in the name of the wizard

and he is asleep in Lincoln's bed
as all mulatto melodies

are slavery's taboo
and white supremacy

it teaches power's selectivity
inoculating all but few

yours but a sacred project
of the book as it develops

negative arboretum
e pluribus unum

Judicial Assignment

As far away as Greenville
    we call ancestors from elsewhere:

you are on assignment
    in the *annals*

traipsing at Furman
    for written traduction

when most history worth knowing
    is seldom recorded;

now you must build up
    honorable amendments

(resisting the resonant
    e-mail

even from the street
    as you prepare your archives

for the John Hay Library
    right next to Lincoln);

in the next century
    your own jurisprudence

will ensnare pioneers
    in many thickets

and tales will be told
    in marginalia

including recipes
    where all artistry begins;

a feeding frenzy
    over the Natchez Trace

once a Chickasaw trail
    now a scenic highway

is Rhode Island law;
    the periodic table

is balanced
    in your opinions.

for Ojetta Rogeriee Thompson

Advice to Clinton

Re race rituals look up Elaine,
Arkansas; for race relations

let John Hope Franklin
lead you into *his* orchid

field; outside of Tulsa,
during the 1921 bombing

raid on Greenwood,
all tribal outposts

in the territory
were half Stand-Watie

half Crazy Horse:
agitation over race

is our national hothouse:
glass all around us;

birds and bees
pollinating

above the color line
and use the kerosene

dropped from planes
as border ruffians

came into Lawrence,
Kansas, to kill a dozen

white men
on a short list;

meanwhile, defenseless
black recruits,

caught in rivergrass
were slaughtered,

without any arms.
You must explain

(even in cyberspace)
the Elaine riots:

who rioted:
take the country

to the woodshed
as Confederacy

amidst Union:
this is orchid country:

bombing raid
succor

new flowers
bud and bouquet:

(bind up the nation's wounds)
hear the nation scream

prune and preen
hear the nation scream

Patrice Lumumba

Leopoldville
is the acid
of the day;
the incised line
cuts surfaces
over the stones
of the savannah

Kinshasha
photographs
the prophet king
in Katanga

in Brussels
a black
cannot go home
foretelling
what Europe is

the catholic
principles
(black soldiers
white officers)

haunt museum
assassins

Mobutu
staggers
in champagne

trains
of handless
corpses
light
trolley
lines

urania
pillage
banana

Belgian
francs
Sabena
beliefs
coded
messages

30 6 60
Belgian
Congo
still
Conrad's
Intended

Reading Jean Toomer's *Cane* Again

"For news of the heart consult the face."
—Proverb

Your lemon face delicious
and for the asking

if the cadence
is correct

(biblical
student of the psalms

crass analogies
at the edges

of race and sex
concubines

the factories:
cannibalism)

"Silence
too   is talk"

Your ancestors
raw meatballs

sinews
of dynastic order

and no payment
that is not psychic

display
the color of your eyes

amalgam
exquisite

"the years do not fall
on the ground

but on the body"
words deeper than tears

FREDERICK DOUGLASS CYCLE

THE LOVE LETTERS OF HELEN
PITTS DOUGLASS

When I stood behind his desk chair
and when he sat, on rare occasions,
on the porch, "sage of Anacostia,"
they called him, I smelled his mane
glorious, and as a hand saddle
the aroma of hair took me to neckline
and below. In Egypt, long after
Napoleon had shot off the face
of the Sphinx, I thought of this
man, and the cusp of his palms
on my shoulder blades;
as always he was carrying the mail
of gender, his touch immaculate
in the true blend of the cortex,
and of the complex, risen on a pulpit,
and after the hot air, wintry parlance,
the syllables of my name in his ear,
when he touched me, as he had touched
me then.
       I had my suspicions of English
ladies, actresses, ghosts of the Thames,
concubines, as we had been into this next
century. And they had their wiles with him.

I do not feel forbidden; the cameo ring
he gave me, recession of his maleness
all I need, and highlights of my dark
profile, any children we might have
had buried in architecture,
and the hate of his daughter Rosetta,
who I have spoken to over the grate.

The sun rises and sets in our neighborhood:
I WILL BURN THESE. But when I place my fingers
in that mane it is to the saddle he will come.

THE DOUGLASS POSITION, 1863

I was promised a commission;
from his very lips
the confederacy

prevented me from Vicksburg,
able recruits, blacker than berries,
were eatable, and the machine ate;

Grant would know of this,
or knew, even over maneuvers,
what was best;

we two shared a gallon of brandywine
and gave it to recruits,
and saw their faces turn

in the Crater
and knew the victory of killing
with impunity, and wishing it so.

John Brown came to me;
he ate, swiftly, or at leisure,
at my table, and talked of

Harpers Ferry
as though rivers,
and the reality of embankments,

were weapons in the hands
of Shields Green.

I could not go; the testing ground
of Antietam was very much
in letters he could not write,

yet, he wrote openly
to his son about how to traverse
the Ohio River at flood stage

as guidelines to Owen,
who was bringing arms to Kansas.

Kansas was my undoing with my fellows;
what I could see of leaving home burial
ground, the cemeteries of our tongues,

was to repeat the ravaging of the Indians,
who had preceded us,
on the continental shelf.

Rugged men on the prairie
and left alone to raise benevolent
grass for the explorers,

but settlements in segregation
when all needed work, jobs,
newspapers, books:

you could draw the childish pictures
for the presidential children,
and like the madhouse waiting

for Mrs. Lincoln, across the White
House street: there was the cane,
and the caning. This was given

to me instead of commission:
because I chose to lead men and women.

THE HIDDEN FRIENDS OF
FREDERICK DOUGLASS

On the maternal side of our family
there were eavesdroppers and John

Bowers was from Massachusetts; he went
to sea as a young man—there was no mention

of parents or family, but he was a whaler
out of New Bedford; while at port he met

and married Henrietta Smith in Baltimore
or Philadelphia; they resided in Philadelphia;

she had thirteen children. John Bowers
was a delegate to the National Negro Convention;

he ascended to the presidency after the death
of Richard Allen; he was warden of St. Thomas Church,

a trustee of the Day school, founded in 1804
for the teaching of our young people. He was

a tailor by trade, catering to elite clientele.

Henrietta was a maker of coats, cloaks, and capes;
when her husband died she was determined

to take over his undertaking business;
passing all the tests she became the first

talk of the bodies of friends, neighbors,
strangers never passed her lips;

her brother, Thomas Bowers, was the finest
singer of his day, compared with the great

Italian tenor, Mario: we called him "The Colored
Mario"; he was steadfast in his stance

not to perform before segregated audiences;
one evening, in Hamilton, Ontario, a Dr. Brown

purchased six first-class tickets, reserved
seats, and on arrival was refused admittance.

Colored Mario refused to perform; management
acquiesced; "no colored" in first class ended;

the performance was brilliant.

Henrietta gave Frederick a coat made to Anna
Murray's measurements; he laid out

in hand-felt sketches of her curvatures
a pattern for a coat, and brought it home

in a handmade carriage made by a blacksmith
in Hamilton. The documents of affection

in the unwritten rules of protection
were sketched out in those conventions:

these were family matters; some ties too solemn
and hurtful at separation to be mended with thread:

literacy is a very tender thread in America,
and it is threadbare on race and sex:

the problem of the twenty-first century
are the avenues of miscegenation;

the grievances of feud and family
are these patterns of coloration,

this menagerie.

PREACHING AT THE FUNERAL
(SONGS OF THE CHOIR IN SILENT PRAYER)

My father was a quartermaster in the British
Merchant Marine; of Scot descent he married

my mother, Mary MacKay, daughter of the chief
of the Chippewas of Dalhousie; they had but one

child, John Albert Johnson, born in Oakville,
reared as an Anglican, converted to Methodism

while a student at the University of Toronto;
his degrees included the M.D. in medicine,

and while celebrating, wasting the Lord's
time in revelry, he was chastised by an old

woman about leaving "His" work undone.

Two years in British Guinea as a medical missionary
took him to Queens College, Oxford,

for another master's; with ordination
in the African Methodist Episcopal church

he was itinerant minister in St. Johns,
New Brunswick; his circuit took six weeks to traverse;

then he was assigned to Hamilton, Bermuda:
his diary of events, travels, and travail,

raising funds for the church, his ministerings
in England and Scotland, having been refused

service at common dining halls, tending the sick
in Bermuda, is the only record of the daily life

of an AME clergyman. His entry on the end of monarchy
in Brazil, 1888, is too precious for recitation,

and resides in the Schomburg, his son's best friend,
who was outcast for his black Puerto Rican patina.

"He was not a gangster bishop," and his words
in the 1924 convention at Louisville

were manly in the extreme, such eloquence
snuffed entirely by jealousy, exile to South

Africa, the silence of the American Negro Academy,
and minutes at Wilberforce, with other semiliterate

divines; he was a director of Douglass Hospital,
Citizens & Southern Bank, the Pioneer Building & Loan

Association, all of Philadelphia: his picture hangs
in the rectory at Mother Bethel. An Odd Fellow

and Mason, he holds the LL.D. honorary degree
and wrote the citation for brother Douglass.

Men of high quality, action, and thought
never apart, Senegambian and negrito,

sallow in the field; they rise up as trees
in the oak forest of mettle, and sing

in the blossoming, and they are cut down.

Look up the scientific matters of the Upas tree
that bedevils our ministries, our educators,

our husbandry and wifery, and ask for strong stools
at kinder and at garten, and at the gravesites

if you can find them: and find them you will
everlastingly. Power concedes nothing without demand.

MEDITATION ON AUBURN PRISON
(FOR HARRIET TUBMAN)

Invisible ink, and purple namesake,
all the prisoners in the library,

smoke so heavy only an asthmatic
can breathe, the shallow sacs

of the bronchial now green
as the starch in those shirts,

pencils forbidden,
all of us locked in

for a solid three hours,
and my three books,

interpretive autobiographies—
"geography is fate"—Heraclitus—

and so I talked of events:
killings I had seen

in the fragments of letters
from the 54th, my own sons

broken on the pantry of employment,
which they could not get;

for the sake of education,
which I never had

and could have bought if I could
beg my rivals, my son went

without, and my daughter went berserk
with her sister's death,

and their mother unable to dive/frolic/spin
in the rhetoric of the pen

though she should write her memoirs
beginning in Lynn, New Bedford,

and the fires of Rochester
by neighbors, by friends.

I got my fees; the politics of Washington,
a plantation in flight,

what Booker and the Carnegie machine,
what George Foster Peabody

would collect in his private annals,
pleas for intervention against lynching:

this would continue.

I spoke to the inmates about Huntington,
railroad man, and Gould, more than railroads,

and the spirit of N. Elba, N.Y.,
where the whole family of John Brown

levitates behind the iron fencing;
I asked for a place in that crypt

if justice be done to runaways,
and found the feathered resistance

of self-creation the only American lesson,
and beneath the rhythm of bondage

my own father's white supremacy
just behind the beat,

even in Lincoln's "Second Inaugural,"
which I, hunting for metaphor,

helped him to write, the hunt for true
metaphor in a one-dimensional world:

and from the pulpit, black messianic visions
"it was a sacred effort."

"FREDERICK, IS GOD DEAD?"

Two lions astray on the mission,
as if to agitate was part of disposition,
as if to amplify and extend

constitutions, the short intestines
of fire-eating animals,
with manes, teeth,

and the killing tree,
which is always a legal
penitentiary: Auburn prison.

Hidden graves: markers as subtle as pig,
wagon, woods, Covey, and coveys in praxis

from Invisible Man to Cedar Hill:
the question is who are you?

and in serious trouble
when you cannot even talk to your mother

Cuffy's wretchedness and Severn's blood
in the battle-ax of the republic.

Whites, who loved Greek names,
knew the Greeks were slaveholders,
and Egypt was just monotheism,

where the godhead imploded
on the desert, over water,
under the golden stool.

The songs of Aunt Hester, water-wading
forbids the head shot,
for the mind resides there,

and the mind knows the law
as Constantine did, so reading
a spelling book is lionine.

For the rest of your life you study
the preachments of Nat Turner,

knowing, in Hayden's ballad,
that something is predicted,

but all the sermonizing is before
rebellion: the target of repression,

even the Civil War,
is my religion for the rest of my life.

I enjoyed writing my own pass,
and those of my fellow runaways,

and, since practice makes perfect,
I came to understand why literacy

in the mouth of the poor, domesticated
whites, was villainy,

and watched it wrested upon me.
Garrison, who had a lisp, and hated

to be mimicked, wanted to write my pass,
and so we parted; you must be cunning,

even in the midst of your friends,
and wary of secret societies,

which white men harbor in the vestibule
of auricles and ventricles. Heartblow!

We are asked to be individuals;
at Nantucket I came to know my own
stammer, symbol and causality as hired gun,

the portfolio the scars at welcome-table,
in jim crow accommodations,
touch and talk in England,

the "levels of difficulty"
the extremist news of the ear:
white paranoia.

When talking to women
there was gentrification;

on July 5th I stood on the levy,
as the slaves did,

with the everlasting
monsoon; that song was the song

I sang on the levee
at news of Annie's death,

and at Harpers Ferry.
Even in New York,

seat of the draft riots,
all my Irish blood came home to roost.

I dreamed of the Federal Arsenal;
I knew I could be Delaney

with the brains of Robert E. Lee
but wanted my commission

for hidden indictments,
troop gathering from Jeff Davis's

legions of the will-be,
for the past was in Charleston harbor,

and I was happy for that war of necessary
carnage, with us paying for the highest price.

And the willingness to pay:
honorable amendments, all I ask for

in the future; heartbreak in the Freedmen's
Bureau, and my house burned down

by WS men, all unapprehended,
the criminals known to the judges

in my adopted hometown:

Mr. Lincoln's gadgetry for whites only;
the Hayes-Tilden Compromise signed

in a colored hotel, Congress Hall:
this is parlor talk for Anacostia,

the bighouse of opinion of a self-made man:
Booker writing what Willie should have written:

I dreamed I was lynched, regaining my voice,
by my actual parents: and Anna said:

marry a younger woman, start a whole new family,
make smoke come out of Rosetta's nose.

And Harriet came to remind me of four hundred souls
I got to Canada; Sojourner, in her native Dutch,

drowned in holy water at masculine pitch by candle.
As Bishop Johnson said: you are awaft

at the shrine of miraculous cures: a white man's bedstead,
your forgiveness; all answers from Isis gathering spent parts.

DREAM: BICENTENNIAL, ROCHESTER, N.Y. (AFTER F.D. RESIDENCE FIRE)

Brazil: a continent of exchanges: the quilt
sewn together by Pennsylvania women

of another age, was only sewn together by them:
and made three quilts from a box of pieces

found after her death, Methodists all,
those sewers, an underground railroad station,

a whole continent of aborigines
in a rain forest of medicines

and in the unnamed trees an umbrella of spices.
A woman is typing my first book

learning the rhythms that cannot be learned
except by process, her secretariat wage

a marriage of quiet cadences,
the research given up in her/his bed

on the circuit, Frederick Douglass
floating in the understory of trees

and in these memories of Maryland everglades
a rhetoric of motives, sanctions,

epiphanies. Later a statue
she has taken me to

astride with waterline
to sop out his ancestral-house-fire.

The poet's great-grandfather wrote down
in his Bermuda journal: 1888: end of monarchy!

He was Canadian; his father a quartermaster
from Guyana; mother, daughter of a chief

of the Dalhousie; carousing on the Toronto
streets, celebrating his medical school exams,

he was sent out to America,
logged the coming and going of ships

and their cargoes: visited with the poor,
put down his flute, his vestry kinsmen

and put his deeds up in the ministries
of Mother Bethel. No jackleg bishop he.

Trustee at Wilberforce; had friends in Alma,
Michigan; preached at the Louisville convention: 1924.

No gangster bishop he; the "amens" in his diocese
were all the documents we ever needed, preacher man.

FIGMENTS

How shall the mind keep warm
    save at spectral
fires—how thrive but by the light
    of paradox?
—Robert Hayden, *Stars*

He had the head to conceive,
and the hand to execute.
—Frederick Douglass, *The Heroic Slave*

Of deep successful love there is ominous silence, and in one of the oldest
of these songs there is a depth of history and meaning.
—W. E. B. Du Bois, *The Souls of Black Folk*

The Iowa River but tributary:
(on both sides of the sacred grove)
in the afternoon blighted sun

a pale pregnant Finnish woman
slipped into the breaks
of transparency

on the Art Bridge,
late for prenatal care,
her husband locked in mortal

elegies of the doctorate.
I help her up from her knees
and anklets, stop the first

hawk-eyed insigniad
snowmobile, hurry her to
an outpatient side door

near the back stairs of the quarters.
When I see her in foliage
on Washington Street

she dances behind the female
carriage, her husband half-nelsoned
beside her; the sidesaddle follicle

elms introduce me to her daughter,
for the first time asking my name:
this is perhaps Edwin Arlington Robinson's plight

in the big apple written in gold
letters in the downcast eyes
of Cecil Rhodes, *An African*

Slaver manual the manuscript
you have to carry on maneuvers,
your manicured army dispatch case

the real story of Hampton, Virginia,
town and gown and the Indians.

Mr. Washington off the coast of New
Orleans, behind the sacred phalanx
of trees, the creole *gaubees* shaken

backwards and forwards in pennants
of the everglades,
the military cache of Stand Watie's surrender:

> It is a little known fact that many
> black soldiers who served in the *first*
> *second* Kansas Colored units
>
> were natives of Indian Territory
> who had fled north, were living
> in Kansas refugee camps along with those Indians
>
> who were sympathetic to the North.

Praise to Pocahontas and the underwater
tunnels of the mines, incident at the Crater.

"Dear Madison Washington:
I am in the midst

of research on Stand Watie and his Confederate
Indians and the black towns of Oklahoma;

the collections are good, the stuff
on Stand Watie mind-blowing, so much

literature written by rednecks,
Klan-types with weird ideas

about mixed-blood vs. full-blooded Indians.
Stand Watie's mother was half-white,

a member of the Moravian church;
her father, Uweti, was Cherokee.

Son was brigadier general,
last Confederate to surrender.

His name stands for either "to stand
immovable," or "two people standing

closely together as to form one
human body": the terms are "Ta—ker—taw—ker"

and "De—gata—ga." Which one do you think
has more interesting connotations?

More often only part-white Indians
fought for the Confederacy; full-blooded

Indians for the Union. Many Cherokee
and Creek Indians were segregationists;

the greatest foe to these segs
was Chief O—po—th—leyo—ho—lo—he had a small

following of Seminoles as well.
(this is in the wrong state, of course, Oklahoma, not Virginia)

The fight, in the WPA annals, boils
down to land for blacks; some white Scottish

slaveowners from Georgia
pushed west and Jefferson Davis

sent Albert Pike into Indian Territory
to get help from the mixed-bloods

of the Five Civilized Tribes. The Cherokees
split down the middle, North and South.

Why is there always quotidian *land*—
I swore northern Virginia was as far

as I'd ever go; in the Tidewater
the blossoming voices behind the Emancipation

trees are full of abolitionists (Indians once more near the sacred grove),
their dutiful enactments of race and religion.

Handling any of Bob Hayden's poetry now
I'd focus on the religious,

and on the Indians, in their shades
and scarecrow feats of miscegenation.

Thank God for Dr. Du Bois
and his relatives in New Bedford and New Haven;

he had the pilgrim's fascination
with the architecture of the grave,

and of the souls of black folk archive,
and I meditate on that against Chicago's

Park School of Socioethnicity
the Panzer critics of the day:

with Gunnar Myrdal holding up at Princeton
all through the war

without shibboleth before it;
though he did see Harlem.

P.S.: Other than your poetry,
your posturing is for the students,

literate facts the obscure bloodlines
and our hue and cry; you sound

so pure in the postmodernist amnesia
of the workshop. Burn this, don't save.

For postnatal coitus of the traditional
narrations of the river and the tribe.

As you went under:
the border wars of the American Dream

never speak in the forked idioms
of cant at Calhoun; great piano music.

I bless you first for Bob Hayden's
tears in the penultimate shadowed
refrains; laugh at the ultimate.

The three black boys who swam the Iowa
River, not far from the Art Bridge
on a hot spring day—one of them drowned—

told by his white classmates
the river was never more than four
feet of water: trusted that speculation.

As the creek does rise
no one cries nullification
as John Calhoun's ghost hurries for home.

Your middle name's Du Bois's connection
to crusading locusts blanketing
the schoolmarms learning to read.

Hayden's Bible circuit reading tour
of Virginia ends up in chapel,
at lunch, did Charlie grow up here?:

(he has in mind the true mythology
of original experience in the forest,
society's nonmethodical ethnic dream)

what would have happened to me
had I grown up in Altoona
where my mother was born

instead of the underground station at Detroit.

You wince at the early Sunday
MLA session, here my commentator
goes on about membership

until he's sabotaged
some spectral annotations;
said, Michael, I have to

take you to dinner,
wash the stench
from the margins of your papers:

ate French food that night,
best I ever tasted in the city.
And Jeanne was always lovely.

Your military brogans
come and go
in the World War II

army correctives,
dress rehearsals
learned about the lexicographer—

never gave up dreams
of writing plays with Robeson
and Du Bois in mock debate,

the score Ellington,
the choral sections
modulations

on African affairs.

Paterno sat with me at table
his honorary Brown degree
long gone in reveries of the gridiron;

said he liked your style,
data and documentation, white on rice,
confused your tongue with Fritz Pollard's

family, said you didn't look alike though.

What do you know of the Negro Leagues,
you asked: of Willie Mays from Birmingham's

suburbs of the steel mill, rewrote
DiMaggio, played against the Bushwicks

one Sunday, had that marvelous laugh,
shuck and twinkle of the pennant chase;

how much tennis black folk played
at homecomings in Old Dominion

no longer mattered after Blackjack
and the Dodgers. Not to mention Joe Louis in the stadium.

Demand your books in the Schomburg;
he ate too much chicken in your grand-
mother's kitchen to keep you out;

tell my son about Coltrane
so he can get back to his scores
and books. (*That is right!*)

Treating writers best
one by one, you see the process

in the slider, rising fastball
of a shifting point of view;

Stanford's not as picturesque
as Lake Como; no Ishmael

you understand, no gumbo either.

Mr. Douglass's statue in the city
park in Rochester is near a railroad

all the way to Chatham, Ontario;
the white girl who asked

wanted to avoid the falls.

When Richard Wright's daughter
came to Calhoun with her mother,

said: tell Mr. Davis that my father
was never the Frenchman

they said he was; perhaps
was the happiest in Brooklyn,

where you were born—
couldn't get into England

when I went to school,
couldn't get out of France

when he had to, 1960:
cried over Sharpeville;

knew more than he wrote down.

Have you ever read *Paterson*
without the stanza breaks

and legends; not the city,
the thing itself:

couldn't find a single
true black voice in that taut prose.

Nor in St. Elizabeths either.

Tell your mother, the witch doctor,
she has comely daughter,

reminds me of Barlow's
wife; Barlow said her father

thought you looked just like his dead
son; that telegram Jeanne and I

sent to St. Paul
was meant for more than you—

it speaks to the struggling
tongue of all our ancestors:

tell this to my grandson—
don't let the students in the program

see unwritten letters
of my purple prose

unless they have degrees,
conscious act upon act,

deed upon deed:

remember me always in the imagination
where I wrote my best play

upon the Mississippi River:
the sacred World's Fair, St. Louis, 1900.

Eliot hadn't gone to England;
Twain was twain,

and Frederick Douglass—
he created characters such as me—

for Charles Twichell Davis, in memoriam

If You Don't Force It

tie your left hand behind your back
then play the melody with one finger

on your right hand:
put the melody on your heart

If You Don't Force It

He's talking about interpolations
riffs that come in the midst

of action, responding to the line,
accommodating the blues

and note neglecting the melody
refusing to smother beauty

with too many chords
to show off is to bungle

the melody with chordal blocks
not building anything to your baby

hiding the melody
like only the young can do

Lester Young would watch the dancers
moving into his vernaculars

with rhythms augmenting the melody
Herschel would set the pace

Pres would follow
Count would comp time

as though you could improve
on stride piano

Ben Webster could do stride
when you get possessed with wild chords

tie your left hand behind your back
then play the melody with one finger

on your right hand:
put the melody on your heart

    for Ray Brown

Audio

In the *buzzard's roost* sonics
their equipment even at these registers

imperfect, the gloss of sound
off the charts in Mor Tiam's

agitations; John Hicks on ivories,
Phillip Wilson on skins, Wadud on cello

the Fort Worth train tracks of your birth
a fine demarcation of segregation

Dexter Gordon's comment, at seventeen,
on his first gig with Hampton's band

The temple of St. Louis is the river
the arch into the wilderness

a band of Indians alive
in the Blue Devils Band

this territory is more than Bessie Smith's
and it contains the Tulsa riot

when Greenwood was burned to the ground
from the air from that smoke and kerosene

your lips approached the *dogon*
glottals of *Bird* and *Trane*

the *Hard Blues* the only artistry
of this sleepwalking country

stealing from the best
rewarding no one

outside of performance
A bomb threat emptied

1,800 paid ticket-holders
from *Powell Hall*

as the *African Continuum*
vaulted on the bass line

of the ancestors
ghosts with instruments "always" playing.

in memoriam, Julius Hemphill, 1938–96

Matchbook: The Spinnaker (Sausalito)

Adrift in your own spittle
(eyebrows on vibrato knuckles)

we are across the bay
from reality;

but reality hits in waves
and Tatum weaves

into the picture:
Pittsburgh, Bill Basie

filling in
until the man arrived.

There will be no talk
of mechanics

the smack direction
enough for any master's

fingers, and the wrists
are flexible

as any girl's;
the speed limits

on the bridge
are foggy

and out of gear:
T-birds, Mercedes

roll off Tiburon;
Mill Valley

is the papaya
of Vietnam;

French music
in your appreciation

is orchestrated
around Dien Bien Phu

because of the craft
of the French:

Pres and Bud
only alive

for awhile
because of it:

in memory of Bill Evans

On First Listening to *Native Dancer*
by Wayne Shorter

Brazil voices
are not like any other:
a woman you can't sleep
with crooning about rivers

the morpho caught
in the canopy

real people live
in the rain forest

Sacrifice:
having lyrical gifts
to lead an aesthetic
assault on the pulse

but not the stomach
for the marketing

every piglet to market
for the eating

Amazon carnivores
are more than women
on the hunt

soprano Christendom
with the spears/amulets
of indigenes

you can never get over

a sacred friend
from Trinidad
provided this lesson
in Hindustan:

make your own path
in the night

every mountain dew
is the breath

of the mother

her blessed child

papa singing
a cappella

to his library

unwritten books
of the unseen

Relaxing with R.B.S. over Tunes

Too many ferry rides in my past to make book
on any passage; too much *Amistad*
mutinous interiors, too much grief,
too much dross, keepsakes fondle elements
as fish to water and Pip speaks
nothing in the brine; Bishop Johnson
with his Johnson lungs, bought Evaton
for our kinsman near Sharpeville,
his first building at Wilberforce
a woman's dormitory, a case-hardened
armature of spirit only praisesongs
possess; in his Bermuda journal of 1892 (1888)
he mused on the end of monarchy in Brazil
and slavery became dross avenues of the mind.

We live there, with Nefertiti; in Alexandria
once I ate the best shrimp in the world
just off the train from Cairo; then taught
the *Souls* to Ethiopian refugees who'd been
tortured: hook line and sinker they were en route
to D.C., to work cab, do maps, matriculate
at Howard, take the long walk; I told them
it was a mystery why bloods in the States
did not hate them, as they took the ready
jobs on the ferris wheel at Union Station.

Sterling told a joke about Sam Jones
puttin' on dog for the redcaps, signifyin'
about to miss his train; Brer Sterling
had a gloss for possum and Lady Day
in St. Elizabeths; please remember Douglass
uninvited after A. Lincoln's "Second Inaugural":

"it was a sacred effort"; in writing "memoirs
of your sires" in and out of Hyde Park
it is fresh space we need on natal days;
let it be squid who have no hiding place
except the ink of protection: let us pass.

My Mother's Bible

No one wrote like her,
each one of her children

on its own page,
births, deaths,

marriages
held together

by a royal ribbon
and an anchor

from her grandfather
the bishop

who forbade her from playing
jacks on the sabbath;

made her come indoors,
though proud to walk her

up Layfayette Avenue
under the chestnut trees,

her bonnet
framing the Braxton nose

and the Johnson lungs.
In the year of the tiger,

1938
in the Chinese calendar,

I was born
thirty-three hours in labor

delivered by her father
with two dogs running

under the bed:
"look, he's marked for papa"

Dr. Johnson said
about the mole on my right

shoulder;
and I watch the mole

in my sixtieth year
for enlargement,

discoloration,
a keloid, a recessive hair

as one is fricasseed
in the holding tank

of the family pantry
where one does laundry

or scullery work
or tells the story

of missionary work
in the veld

before the Union
was the Union.

I took this book
to the Transvaal

and out of Africa
to Latvia,

onto the Natchez Trace,
into Tuscaloosa

"on green dolphin" street
our favorite psalm.

Arrival

Some love to be lost, Redford said so, in film
and gave away his compass; I take compassion

seriously, find my way without proper bearings
trust little, containing my anger over time and place

to the third grade when police from my own borough
took me to New Lots and let me out without a beating

and without a nickel; ten years later I peered
in a microscope looking for somites in nematodes

and was told by Dr. Bell there was no point
to premedicine for me; it was not possible.

The Jew in the class, George Siegel, was told the same;
we got together at the count, biding our time on somites.

Soon after I was assaulted with my brother by three Irish
Indiana ruffians in a short stay in my borough

they tried running me off the road; I was reading Milton
at ULCA Library on the eleventh hour, eleventh month

eleventh exegesis of *Paradise Lost*, long before Milton's Cottage
locked up in Rimpau Station with a failed 33d degree Mason

on a warrant; four days I refused to talk with him,
my brother in an adjacent cell out of earshot

assault with a deadly weapon, without bail over the holidays;
I had no remorse; flash of ironing board, steamiron

two ran, before arraignment the true elemental
chance to choose, do it again, was upon me

when the man with a plate in his head
said the magic word, "nigger," once more

Jonathan begged me to put him down
as I arched my back to loft him out

of the seventh floor judicial foyer
to stalagmites below; I put him down.

Marvin Harwich, for $1,000, got them to drop
charges as we paid hospital fees and we walked free.

A version of the real story; pie inside
tenderhearted, and beige in the yard with teddy

I would throw him down the stairs
then caress, cajole, and do it again

my grandma's backyard full of roses,
thorns in the wick and ember of patrols

was this ever home, when Charles Japangy, the Wibecans, Frank Kelly
waited with Nits, Jollystompers, White Fence, Watts Locals,
South Park, Amboy Dukes, Blackstone Rangers, and their paramours,
lieutenants, ombudsmen, gobetweens, female mainsqueezes
lollypoppers, lockerroom attendants, fencebenders, aids on line
jumped to attention to offend you, to trash, intimidate, beat
into silence, cunning, postwarsyndromicpsychosis.

I was born in the same house as my mother, and delivered by the same
    man.
how strange this configuration of the chestnut tree
how delicious the radiant nut; hurricane of 1948:
all the trees on Lafayette Avenue blown
then cut down; the Elks, who came to pay tribute
to my grandfather, his body laid out on cooling board,
paraded down the ample street,
and one patient-admirer-customer,
who called him "my seal brown,"
was ushered into the waiting room
and told by my grandmother, Alice,
"you can have him now!"

This was 1940. I was "marked for papa"
he said on home delivery,
and Trigger, the Pekingese,
ran back and forth under the birthing bed;
the mole on my right shoulder
marks the spot: love your blemishes.

My grandpa and great-grandpa were born on the same
October day, papa on my mother's birthday
took to the cooling board; Alice said he sleepwalked
and was gentle being brought back to bed
perhaps remembering Bermuda
when his father preached and ministered
to the poor; when his ship finally came in
a roster of gentlemen from Exeter
were on the gangplank;
whatever happened to the M Street crowd
is pure guesswork,

and to be guessed at:
"seal-brown," and black with rage
at the Armory Show when he was questioned,
an accurate color tintype his exact coppertone,
he promenaded at the reservoir,
courting my grandmother,
before Fifth Avenue had its public library,
and both of them trustees
having been married in St. Phillips Church
which bought apartments for the affluent
of color, in Harlem, before it was fashionable
to own property, a purchase of self
if and when you were freed from Canada
where you were born but could not live:
this was the reverse geography (fable)
of the above-ground railroad
taking your relatives to Minnesota
from one reservation to another
Ojibwa to Chippewa
what's the difference;
in the homelands,
at the watershed
at the source
boundary waters
of the Mississippi
you cast your lot
with "the people"
in spiritual terms
and waited, defending
what you were,
or took to the word
of your fathers
and put meat to metaphor
delivered your own children,
breech or no breech,
you turned your offspring
around in the womb
to bring them back alive.

Cinco de Mayo

My mother's favorite holiday;
she loved Mexican silver

wearing the dress of the natives
with homemade avocado soup

from a huge tree that grew in the yard;
my brother would rope the world in it

cursing out the next-door neighbor
who had driven his cat up her tree

with a hose; fearless
and without repeating himself

a litany of curses wafted
into the blossoming avocado

he also born in May
in the sweet fragrance of ether

all his own, vapors of gasoline
from his Yamaha probably killed him

as he raced to the aid of a child;
my mother sang an aria

from *Tristan and Isolde*
in Wagnerian calm

a calm of the broken-hearted;
she had once taken a contract out

on my sister's husband (a Marine)
but did not execute her will

before he went over Mulholland Drive
in a Hillman/Morgan sports coup

and I spent a bad day in Tijuana
on my eighteenth birthday

three speeding tickets, one parking
before the trip to Cerveza and girls;

Girls young as angels
their ancient eyes luminous

as Cortés and Montezuma
on Sundays in the Zocalo

The summer Coltrane died
was my last trip to Mexico

the bullfight in Mazatlán
during the Asian wars

nightfall in the wash
of border crossings infinitive.

Homage to Mamie Owens

Only once did I see you
in Catskill; there were stories
of your temper, how you could
not read, even in Hell's Kitchen
you turned out the brood
in regiment
          and could fight like a man.

It is that *man* I address
                on St. Paddy's Day
1998; you have been dead
              all these years
and I remember my brother, Jonathan,
might have learned to curse from you,

that his bloodline, not extant
in the local cemetery,
           was deadly;
his ashes are dispersed
            in the waters of Long Beach

while yours are in the graveyard
              which has its own
brand of segregation;
          only my aunt,
born here and now in Florida,
            and Father Murphy
in his cups on this day
          at the rectory rest
could lead me to Aunt Cora
          born in Hudson

before the bridge
                  was on anybody's drawing board.

She cooked for all the Catholic nuns
and hated her own kind
                  but loved Ed Harper
because he was cousin to a leprechaun,
gangster elf, and scary, of all but his wife,
and the "coffee pot hot five," who played
in a net; he too would take off for the bicycle
races, and pass for an elf with a cigar,
and secretly love the Brooklyn Dodgers
owned by O'Malley, and granting privileges
for all local concessions.
                      The mob crossed
each side of the Hudson
               for profit.
                     My grandpa
cut ice to make ends meet: his battle royale
was the mandolin, which he could make and play,
and a fight to the finish,
                     which he inherited
from his mother, Mamie Owens:
                   her *punch* I praise
on St. Paddy's Day.

At the Moment

While listening to John Coltrane's "Moments Notice" on NPR

There is hurt and no balm gilead
for St. Jude is my patron saint

the room I was given at monastery
retreat in Esopus, New York,

so I conjured Sean Connery in Chicago
Untouchable on his belly in blood

gasping for his medal
which he hoped would protect him

The view from St. Jude's window
of the Hudson River

is just south of my father's birthplace
and day boats collapse and carouse

in the shallows and deeps
of this polluted artery

to and from salt water
in the Dutch waterways of the New World

which was never new to the Esopus:
Josephus Long's little bug on 9 W to Esopus

in the mainline to New Paltz
and his staggered classes on Wiltwyck's

schedule of drugged and manacled boys
with a 600 school and volunteer Mennonites

all any boy needs when homeless
abandoned   abused   anointed   in herring runs

on the runaway trail to steep medications
team meetings   and records of shrink and caseworker

three at a time batteries in the arsenal
of a schedule so you can get back to the apple

whose eye is family   missing in action
not about to be found   in any monastery

except for St. Jude   every lost cause
in the mercy side   of the New Testament

(Cave Canem Meditation)

Queries to Alice Elizabeth: An Obituary, Palm Sunday, 1998

"Beauty is truth, truth beauty,"—that is all
Ye know on earth, and all ye need to know.
—John Keats, "Ode on a Grecian Urn"

You have not lost your grip on the back nine
the role of caddy beneath you, *I am Elizabeth!*

yet on a chair car from *Chehaw* they drew
a curtain around you at meals

all the way to Brooklyn you could not eat;
didactic riffs from *Fort Huachuca*

a noxious history of race rituals in this world
the wizard dead before you were even born

Tuskegee never way station or homeland,
Brooklyn a trial, the *debs-about-town*

unequal to your vantage point
sidereal time. On East Ninety-seventh

before the trolley tracks on Van Aken
you lead your nine lives as cat-o'-nine-tails

Links in service, and at the bridge
a *melded* cemetery; dross of papa's *boulé* and *comus*

a seal-brown carriage and face-lift in the Elks
your brother, Barrett's, fate at *Four Corners* on *River Road*

at *816* and *902 Lafayette* brownstones
the banquet tables, far and near, at oceanic channels

its cadences lost in rhyme and trope
driving range, driving wheel, *spirit*

only at home in all neighborhoods
God's *zodiac* in vestments beyond the *urn*

We hear the *Amen* corner beyond the *"Johnson lungs"*
habitat in fairway after lake effect

"don't look back, someone might be gaining on you"
a chorus of *Doby, Easter, Brown, Motley, Satchel Paige*

Now with the beloved *Ernest*, both at parade rest,
the girth of your *welcome* table is heavy with roses,

psalms you knew by heart, aslant at *crossword,*
and in the channels, as *vespers,* where you rested.

Rose: May 17, 1998

With no thorn discernible
he lies in his grave in water

he would stand in the yard
among his grandmother's roses

his wavering voice a wafer
from early morning mass

but scratch his delicate surface
and easily the best curser

without an eraser, a tongue
velvet in the asp encore

of hopeless anger;
he spoke, in whispers, to Katherine

his younger sister named for their mother
and she-mother did not remember his birth

anything but natural in 1941
and in 1943 when his sister was born

locked himself in the downstairs
bathroom and threatened to kick it down

the door to any passageway he would transit
in dreams, in curses, in religious instruction

which he did not believe in,
at early mass, at vespers

in the confessional where his penance
was mimicked by nurses and novices

the nunnery of Joyce not yet prescient
on his rosary, his scapula, thornbush

as the rectory paddles would find a seat
but not a blemish on his tongue or posterior

for his talk in dreams was miraculous
his sister answering in the pitch of grace

where no one lived but their epiphanies
were perfume, the rose petals delicious

the aureole of blossom like no other breast
but to suckle every inner sanctum of his world

and hers: across his absence we sometimes talk
witnessing the prosecution of the admiralty: church:

55: The Journey Motif in My Sister's Birthday Song June 6, 1998

I was once in Bergen, Norway,
after a long train ride/ferry

and stayed alone at the terminus
dining alone, with Margaux, royal

as the eyes of Elizabeth Taylor,
who played tennis with me at her club

when I was a boy. Oslo very slow
Norwegians resisting the Germans

like no other Europeans
their eyes lighter than snow

Grieg played his concerto in A minor
for my mother when I was a boy

and I sang it to my sister
Katherine, born during the war

my mother put her into my arms
as she attended her own mother

in successive strokes
written off by every doctor

but my mother who worked with ESP
on the beloved hearing her children

speak to one another in their sleep
in separate rooms, terraces for sight

in the adult years when innocence
was elsewhere: trains from then on

were not significant journeys
elsewhere but music composed in grief

and I saw hers at the piano
she had bought for my father

who hated playing as a boy
practice an agony in Catskill

in an all-white town with no future
he could see until he met her

so I speak to you on your birthday
eleven years to the cadence of lucky

numbers you should have had to play along
with your good looks, your witticisms,

your truth of three parents (me in the count)
and one soulmate whom you talked to in sleepwalk
our lovely brother Jonathan at terminus:

Voice

Philadelphia tonics and tonalities
easy to talk across frontiers

loves the thirties because of Pres
Bean Cootie Rabbit Hawk Lady Fats Fats Fats

loves borders and how to cross them
race free and race therapy by sound

immaculate modulations of F#
won't talk about his love life

at all discipline worked out crossing
Mason-Dixon line and ambivalent

about Harriet Beecher Stowe
liked to land in Kentucky

mostly Lincoln born there
likes his delivery

reading the law instead of study
institutional life bores him silly

took his wife on a ride down Ohio River
as Huck and Jim used to do long ago

refused to read on command
but read widely liner notes by bad

blue note off-minorheadsontunesJohnHammond
conditioned in his disposition

ate up Kansas City music in Kansas
fought the Civil War over Missouri

no Jesse-James-band-ever-traditional
on time in terms of Lawrence-border-ruffian

antics-don't-play-politics-up-river
listened to race records because best

music unrecorded from Chicago to NO
Louis-Pops-Satch-potato-head-blues

please-get-us-some-laxative-Earl-Hines
democratic-music-lover-Bix-wrote-nothing-down

transfixed changes in white black reservation
music in transition 'cross borders

slow lane comics in riots on axes
hones in arkestras elaboration

change the gender Mary Lou Williams
Sassy leading everybody uptempo ala hemp

Shaharazad

A tale within a tale,
framed, fragrant portrait
of the self, at war
with itself,
fantastic in its intricacies
in black and white;
the colors,
botanical
at weddings and funerals,
episodic entries of the wheel,
which is traffic in Watts,
with or without earthquakes,
mud slides, gun battles,
the rigorous protocol
of tactics at cross sections,
streets, projects,
thoroughfares,
and how to survive
entanglements,
which are always
(apotheosis)
life and death.

When my brother, Jonathan,
was alive, you could talk
with him, separated by speech
and distance,
and he would answer:
such truancy, mellifluous
deceit, *oh confidante,*
is more than any marriage,

fraternal equatorial
twins: Gemini and Taurus,
love and its double
in either direction,
the ether of dreamscape
which is the lie:
embroidered truth.

Love Postcard while Listening
to "Autumn Leaves"

My grandpa and his father born on the same day.
When I was born grandpa delivered me after thirty-three hours.

The dogs, Trigger, a chow, and an English setter
stayed under the bed until I cried—

"look, he's marked for papa," my grandpa said,
a mole in the same place as his father.

With that mark went the library I should have had,
which went to the Schomburg and stayed in crates

for decades, and when unearthed sprouted a Bermuda
journal (1892) which John Albert Johnson (from Ontario)

had kept as a working almanac to the coming of ships
and his tending the poor, the "Johnson lungs" my bounty

lungs passed into the generations from the reservation.
The Irish setter has no name I can remember,

but I had a teddy caught in the tintype in Alice's
backyard, the woman who grew the most resinous roses:

folks took them home to splice and prune into books
and perfumes, a blossom that took too much care

to be an Alice, who was named for her grandmother's
youngest, as my mother was named for Alice's mother

new yorkers, virginians, north carolinians, canadians,
guianans, wayfarers, *sea urchins,* chiefs, and indians

catering the strategic needs of dole and hill
passing through the archives of unwritten storm and weave.

"Autumn Leaves" on Blue Note has Miles on Mute
Cannonball's date, Hank Jones on piano, Art Blakey

on drums, Sam Jones, bass: Sam Jones of the famous joke
about missing his train in Union Station in the district:

"my name is Sam Jones, I'm 6'2" long with No. 14 shoes,
and while I'm 'out for lunch' in the colored waiting

room, making a brogan-pass at a geechee waitress
from New Orleans, musician that I am, I done missed

my train." Improvised, the whole set, Cannon's date,
Miles a misnomer, sailing over the leaves to elsewhere.

Elsewhere in the park or median, conjuring relatives
you see, ancestors you can't see, letting teddy,

who took too many train rides up and down the bannister,
too many stairs, stand for the losses, drosses, glosses.

How to Forgive the Father Who Screams at His Son

Fear, and more than fear, how delicate the wings
one needs for flight; it isn't want but *need;*

the ancients reminded us about the wax,
Motown the fare, dancing with no tact for money;

to live in this world you must have time & money,
the hard currency of effects (this is not job-talk);

Jonathan could not stand a raised voice:
don't holler at me, you make me nervous

was his refrain; I heard my siblings
chortle in their tongues in sleep

caressing one another in nightmare:
I learned their speech.

You have a hero's name, two names,
whose increments salute the void

and I will not permit
a fall from grace.

Of course you must find it for yourself,
that space for aerial delights

the fragrance of women who ascend,
they are the complements of the world.

I saw you born near noon in roses,
I saw your perfect teeth

so I know the warrior in this domain,
and elsewhere those attributes that reign:

this is a whisper that you hear at rest
when you sojourned at inner flight upon my breast.

10's & Things

"Fingerings," she says, "a nobody,
intermission pianist
for the likes of Anita O'Day";
but this is Chicago,
three plus years out of Harlem
resisting suicide recommended
by jealous musicians.

Now that you're dead
jockeys begin to vamp
on your treatment
of "'Round Midnight,"
playing it too loud
in the broad daylight
of their swing shifts

in memory of Carmen McCrae

Release: Kind of Blue

Miles (being ahead)
came in early

with the sketches
he did not mention Japanese

visual art
though Bill Evans did

his liner notes
stretching each brushstroke

as metaphor
for playing together

Because you cannot go back
resonance builds

new material
at a recording session

only once
in a lifetime

For these players
five settings

and a figure
who asked of us

to do this
perfectly

as if to play *live*
alone in a group

Miles asked
we answered

A Coltrane Poem: September 23, 1998

"Autumn Leaves" without a bandstand
for your vigorous arc of light

though it is bright and colorful
in the extremities of music

it is no ballad or blues
affixed to the photo album

and we are not in church in fear
of resurrection in vinyl, CD, audiosphere

and Monk is coming back to join Miles
and Bud's "'Round Midnight" is alchemical tribute

"Dear Lord" we have been slowed in our ascension
figurations now energies of another *spiritual*

this very day Mandela spoke in the atrium
of a would-be-government-of-the-tonalities

in tribal speech as in a Babel of taxonomies
of our earthly kingdom now original

and not in amber at the millennium
but of the reed, and father of the reed

When there is no history
When there is no history
When there is no history

there is no metaphor;
there is no metaphor;
there is no metaphor;

a blind nation in storm
a blind nation in storm
a blind nation in storm

mauls its own harbors:
mauls its own harbors:
mauls its own harbors:

sperm whale, Indian, black,
sperm whale, Indian, black,
sperm whale, Indian, black,

belted in these ruins.
belted in these ruins.
belted in these ruins.

To the Reader

My godson, Rafael Stepto, gave me the moniker *Michaeltree*. He was four years old, in 1979, and the riff caught and held; resonance poured forth in the poet's mind and became a filter to a magical conceit.

I had been wrestling with the pietà motif since graduate school at Iowa, and Oliver Jackson, the painter/sculptor, gave me a lithograph he had etched on the theme of the pietà, extending the image in epiphany of Mary and Jesus (surrender and mercy) as an improvisation in the classical mode, by rigorous attention to the line, figurative wholeness, shadow and light, and his own signature in fraternal rendering with full implications of brotherhood, sacrifice, and the mysterious dimensionality of race. The mystery and bifurcation suggests lode, load, and the spirit that accompanies you in both worlds, and the journey between those worlds, the world of manifestation, and the world of the ancestors, an entirely spiritual world, where one has protection by kinship.

While listening to music—Beethoven and Charlie Parker, aka "Bird"—we were at work at the experiential and theoretical level of the Africanness in us and on how to manipulate and control technique with draftsmanlike precision and not betray referentiality, belief, and artistic integrity. We were after a mastery of the representational at the seen, with close attention to the implications of the unseen. The endpoint was artmaking in new imagery whose reference was informed by European aesthetics, but consistent with African modalities and contained in fresh space with no reference other than to its integral oneness. A theory of composition was unfolding for a tough stance on *making*, the production by *force* in artistic rigor that would create imaginative grace where gnosis and being extended the limits of any garden, any map—a dynamic cartography that would extend limits of the imagination.

By family inheritance I was also fully aware of the sermons of my maternal great-grandfather, John Albert Johnson, a Canadian-educated prelate whose Bermuda journal, 1888–92, was the first written account of the daily life of a missionary. One of his first entries, along with the comings and goings of ships and the faith and paltry existence of his patronage, was about the ending of slavery in Brazil (1888) and his questioning of the monarchy as a colonial assumption of control and progress. His sermons remain in the Schomburg Library (Harlem branch) of the New York Public Library, bequested by his son, my grandfather, Roland R. Johnson, to his best friend, Arthur Schomburg, a black Puerto Rican researcher and collector. What was in the public domain should have been in my personal library. As an African Methodist Episcopal bishop John Albert Johnson spent eight years in South Africa, 1908–16, and bought the first freehold land in the British colonies, what became Wilberforce Institute, in Evaton, a stone's throw from Sharpeville. I visited Evaton while on an American Specialist journey to eight countries in 1977: Senegal, Gambia, Ghana, Nigeria, Zaire (now the Congo Republic), South Africa (where I was detained in Soweto, Protea Station), Botswana, Zambia; I also transited Tanzania and Kenya, transiting Liberia on my return trip to the United States. I was given a copy of Alex Haley's *Roots* in Banjul—a signed copy taken from the safe by the USIS officer—and met the griot in the town of Juffure who chronicled Haley's ancestors. I remember reading Sterling A. Brown's 1929 poem "Strong Men" on the University of Zululand campus, which had just been reopened after several months' hiatus because of the national emergency, and a listener approached me after my recitation and asked to see *Southern Road,* Brown's first collection of poems, and the "South African" poem I'd read. He proceeded to copy the poem, in ink on both arms, writing with either hand.

Gwendolyn Brooks selected my first book for publication, *Dear John, Dear Coltrane;* without her I might not have had any public career; this was before I ever met her personally, and I have had the good fortune of knowing pioneering writers: Robert Hayden, Sterling A. Brown, and Ralph Ellison, writers who were visionary keepers of the artistic faith that was never eclipsed by the essential *bravery* of telling the truth with groundbreaking attention to the frontier. The cost of that bravery in social and political terms is still being calculated, but the price willingly paid was an attention to the pressure of artmaking and an allegiance to ancestry as a covenant.

I was also fully aware of my debts to musicians who were pathfinders, with disposition to master convention by extending increment in art and internal growth while fostering wholesome cultural information.

Teddy: in my Chestnut Street loft—a converted jewelry factory built in the late nineteenth century and once called the Hedison Building—is a personal shrine full of Michaeltree associations, many of which are related to my mother, who broke family tradition by being cremated by the Neptune Society in Los Angeles instead of being buried in the Cypress Hills cemetery in Brooklyn. I have a ten-foot cushioned high chair bought from a Yaddo artist with a perch for two teddy bears, one in porcelain bought for my birthday by my mother and a replacement teddy, bought by a friend, on whose lapel rests an honorary Phi Beta Kappa key (Brown University chapter)— a psychic gesture against the hazing I resisted while I was a student in local colleges in Los Angeles and also bought by my mother; a portrait of my parents in the Brooklyn backyard, circa 1937; a few leatherbound tomes for inspiration, including a first edition of *Invisible Man* given to me by a former dean of the college at Brown and signed by the author. There is little comfort in the knowledge that "Teddy" evolved from Theodore Roosevelt's notion that a boy of any age or disposition needed to have a companion. After serving as a psychic conduit for my many adjustments in the world, the "high perch" of a double agent motif is restored to resonant trust.

Notes on Form and Fictions

The title of this book, *Songlines in Michaeltree,* is meant to demarcate the early lessons I learned in Brooklyn, New York, as a child. The safety of my grandmother's backyard filled with rosebushes—hybrids of her own making—still resonates in my memory. Even at this late date I ask myself in the privacy of dreams and remembrance the whereabouts of my proverbial teddy bear.

My mother taught me how to read before I went to school. That first book was the *Arabian Nights,* and soon after my sister was born during World War II I found myself calling her Shaharazad. What I know about my schooling, in the formal sense, in Brooklyn, Los Angeles, and Iowa City is how unteachable I was at every phase of my life. At every juncture, the notion of replication was not in my teachers' field of vision. I learned very early that, because it was a familial given, one could depend only on family for the kind of unconditional love that was a fortification.

I was unteachable because my standards were not generic in the sense of what could be taught in school. I learned more in the post office at Terminal Annex than in seminars on the epic of search, Milton, Eugene O'Neill, literature between the world wars, Whitman, and Dickinson. I also learned a great deal from the minority writers who were closer to my social experience but were not taught systematically in the school curriculum. I read these minority authors independently—free to learn what their gifts were without scholastic structure—though I was sensitive to an emerging tradition of our condition of servitude and the eloquence attached to social restructures and the values inherent in creating one's own values against those restructures. Yeats said, "Memories are old identities"; the identity of an American poet, particularly one with an elongated minority perspective, is a difficult articulation in the experiment of democracy, the worst system of government and clear evaluation, except for all the others.

For an urban child, raised in the first suburb—Brooklyn, New York—born at home as my mother before me, the move to Los Angeles at thirteen was the first breaking of the arc in solidarity. From then on the miseducation of the poet was clearly evident in schooling, in the efficacy of small and large neighborhoods, and in the linguistics of culture, which inhabits all poets.

By *miseducation* I mean to suggest a shifting of zones of poetic discourse. There was something about the nature of metrics that forced an accommodation to the mechanics of the count. So much of my own music was announced to me in the auditory registers of phrasing. The world as I saw it was a cadence of song with speech elements that were fundamental to a theory of increment, a kind of progression that clarified the makings of voice in good and bad times.

From early childhood a certain aptitude with the mechanics of the academic world was seen as a handicap because of the accommodation to a group ethic I could not see, fully explored, except in the imagination. I also had no sense of wanting to belong. The notion of being at home in the world was not a conscious tenet of my development. The journey motif and an articulation of travels inner and outer were my thematics. This is best indicated in the titles of my books.

As a writer who came to an appreciation of literary form I began writing one-act plays that I showed to a visiting writer, Christopher Isherwood, during my undergraduate years. Despite his encouragement, I would not have gone to Iowa and the Writers' Workshop had there been no draft. This was the age of deferment, and I had made up my mind that patriotism, for me, was not expressed in basic training or service in foreign wars. This was an instinctive response to the segregation that was nascent in every familial story I was weaned on. There was an instinctive resistance to authority as well. Had I been able to go to Paris with a newly acquired passport rather than a draft notice I would have felt the contours of expatriation during my early years. I went to graduate school instead. That I was writing both fiction and poetry during this period of my tutelage and reading in the manuscript collection of the university library was a pivotal moment in my development as a writer.

The early 1960s were a promissory note and the first harbinger of a failed notion of freedom and the institutions that needed replenishing over the long haul. I began to write poems because I could not see those elements of my life that I considered sacred reflected in my courses of study: scientific, linguistic, and literary. In the hope of creating fresh space for my majority—those years of maturity that would allow thought and action to become one—I set out on a path to document those elements of contradiction most salient to my antenna and to find a speech that would have some influence on the world I was forced to live in. By every accident and misfortune of this balancing act—the recording of thought and action in the material world—there was an element of luck and an element of foreboding in a kind of progression seen in retrospect.

Against this backdrop, any poetic efforts I have made over the last three decades in formal publications are a barometric reading of the sanctity of family and the miseducation of the poet. The semblance of luck that befell me can be likened to a cocoon made apparent to me, in retrospect, as a magic circle emblematic of the Michael-tree displayed on the back of this book.

A large part of my sensibility has been attracted to the interlopers, outsiders, systematic *makers* who have spent their mature lives producing the *force* that activates the material world with aesthetic energy and a new imagery of possibilities. There is also an element of luck in selecting one's mentors and being chosen by events. I have tried to pay homage to those beacons of light that made living in the world a little easier.

As I look over these poems a theory of increment announces itself in both directions: the past and the future enunciated over themes sacred to me in the arteries of the American tongue. Certain epiphanies underpin the linguistic bank of the poet, and a sense of the story enunciated in phrasing is analogous to the phrasing of the great innovators of classical American music: blues singers, the big band innovations of soloists against a tradition of sonorous social activity. The personalities of musicians and singers in a long tradition of speech and song were emblematic of my private training. I would call this training the training of sensibility. The notion of contending voices—oftentimes musicians at play in the cadences of exchange with an idiomatic speech full of invention and criticism, including self-criticism—was the moniker I attached to what Auden called "memorable speech." I already had a repertoire of articulate kinsmen to use in my work.

After three decades of writing and teaching I have come to appreciate the authority of my own aesthetic disposition in solving poetic and literary problems. There is an inherent arrogance in many of the assumptions of innovative writing at any level of art, but that so many of my examples in the avenues of persona were articulate heroes and heroines and art forms in themselves provided the courage to experiment, to innovate, and not to follow too closely the announced norms. The fresh space necessary for poetic explorations has become, in retrospect, a fountain of ideas that belong to the period of recollection the romantic poets, Keats in particular, announced as "the maintenance of childhood" *connected to the developing man.*

In the best times, when I was fully awake, the act of composition in the making of images was the only point at which I was fully alive. As the poet Sterling A. Brown often said in conversation, "Poetry is not self-expression, the I is a dramatic I." The tree that Michaeltree grew out of is the familial tree of ancestors and relatives who speak to me past and future as muses, voices in a continuum. "Man can embody knowledge, but he cannot know it." The framing of the tale in its most modern treatment is the captive who is free in the mystery of the telling. This is what I have tried to do. "Let the doing be the exercise, not the exhibition."

Notes to the Poems

Dear John, Dear Coltrane

"Brother John" is dedicated to John O. Stewart, fiction writer and anthropologist. The poet was in undergraduate courses with Stewart at Los Angeles State College.

"Alone" was conceived as a ballade and shortened to an aphorism. Miles Dewey Davis is a thematic icon in the poet's development.

"Village Blues" is dedicated to John O. Stewart.

"Elvin's Blues" was written while the poet was reading Robert Browning, particularly his monologues. The choice of idiom is directly related to Elvin Jones's persona as an outsider might envision it, that is, the poet is not a contemporary and not a musician. The use of *narcissus* is meant to meld classical myth and contemporary sociology in the sense that innovative musicians are always on the frontier, rearticulating known and, more importantly, unknown territories. The blues is more important to the poet than painting, in the hierarchy of creative expression.

"For Bud" is a eulogy for Earl "Bud" Powell. Insiders alleged that Thelonious Sphere Monk wrote "'Round about Midnight" so that Bud Powell could play it as it was conceived, with emphasis on the changes inherent in the black keys of the piano.

"Discovery" was the poet's first published poem and was printed in *December* Magazine. The poet read "That Same Pain, That Same Pleasure," an interview with Ralph Ellison, in the first immersion in the Writers' Workshop at the University of Iowa.

"The Black Angel" is the poet's ars poetica as a graduate student. The idea came from Henri Coulette's "Black Angel" poem published in the *New Yorker*. The actual angel was an extension of a mausoleum in a local cemetery in Iowa City. Coulette was the poet's undergraduate teacher at Los Angeles State College. The site of the poem is a local park in the Adams/Crenshaw district of Los Angeles, which he and Coulette shared in the forties and fifties.

"Clark's Way West: Another Version" is an expression of the unwritten lore of Native Americans. Sacajawea, Native American guide to the expedition, assured chroniclers that Clark's slave, York, was literate and conversant in several native languages. According to Native Americans, both Sacajawea and York were personally responsible for the survival of the expedition and its people at several life-and-death decisions of trail and landmarks.

"Remember Mexico" and "Zocalo" are influenced by the kindness of the poet's landlord, Carlos Amador, who owned several houses in the Oceanside neighborhood of San Francisco, a minority outpost in a highly segregated city.

"Black Spring" was the original title of the poet's first collection, *Dear John, Dear Coltrane.* The title was changed because of seeming conflict with Henry Miller's novel/ memoir of the same name. "Spring" in this context is more shale than water supply; it is in the residual of conscious conquest but unconscious possession by bloodlines.

"Blues Alabama" is informed by the rhythms of speech Coltrane appropriated from Martin Luther King Jr.'s eulogy for Addie Mae Collins, Carol Denise McNair, Carole Rosamond Robertson, and Cynthia Wesley, the four black children blown up in the Sixteenth Street Baptist Church on September 15, 1963.

"American History" is a reiteration of the *Oresteia* in the reference to "net," that is, the cyclic unknown history of a new nation repeating the breaking of ancient codes of incest and miscegenation. The concept is indebted to Ralph Ellison's *Invisible Man.*

"Deathwatch" has two resonant debts: W. E. B. Du Bois's correspondence when "experts" on race relations asked him, "Are Negroes unable to cry?" and the refrain of a shoeshiner. "Buck" would mutter "America needs a killing" in response to the wanton comments of the shoe owners in the downtown San Francisco YMCA. They felt free from being overheard amidst a heroic photo gallery—black fighters—as they expressed their unease before "Buck," an archivist and "servant."

"Molasses and the Three Witches" is a play on the *Uncle Remus Tales* as an unexpurgated version of the true resonance and meaning of animal stories of the folk.

"Dear John, Dear Coltrane" begins with a reference to Sam Hose, who was lynched and dismembered in the Atlanta riot of 1906. Both Du Bois and Sterling A. Brown have written poems on this subject. The black church was a haven and revolutionary outpost for uncensored ideas, both of forgiveness and responsibility. "Naima" is a song Coltrane wrote and named for his first wife. It is Coltrane, himself, who is singing.

"A Mother Speaks: The Algiers Motel Incident, Detroit" is an account of the occupation of Detroit, 1967. John Hersey wrote a nonfiction account of some of the incidents in a chronology of incidents and motives. The final utterance in the poem is the actual words reported by one of the policeman as the victim's plea for his life.

"Mr. P.C." is a tune written by John Coltrane for his favorite bassist, Paul Laurence Dunbar Chambers. Chambers, a native of Detroit, was often harassed by gang members in the neighborhood on his way to practice sessions. He died in 1963. Accounts of his life and death are improvised, but short on facts both about his addiction and about his artistry.

"Biafra Blues" is written for the poet's former student at Contra Costa College. Odinochi Nwasu was an Ibo and a college student dislocated from his kinsmen. The poem is meant to suggest the conspiratorial elements of colonialists of the nineteenth century and their twentieth-century apologists.

History Is Your Own Heartbeat

"Love Medley: Patrice Cuchulain" and "This Is My Son's Song: *"Ungie, Hi Ungie"* are poems depicting two brothers—the poet's sons—and their maternal grandmother.

"Here Where Coltrane Is" describes an untimely blizzard in Portland, Oregon, with only a fireplace to heat a large house. The poem shares a title with a recording of a live concert.The poem is meant to suggest the real and imaginary losses and gains of the late sixties.

"Martin's Blues" was written in the idiom of a children's ditty and found a place in the skipping rope games of preadolescents forced to grow up too soon.

"Madimba: Gwendolyn Brooks": "Effendi" and "Madimba" are compositions of the pianist McCoy Tyner. *Effendi* means "wise man," "man of wisdom," or "teacher." A madimba is a hand-played xylophone and also a hair comb for tribal women. The refrain echoes Du Bois's notion of double-consciousness as a practical resistance to white supremacy. The first line of defense against these "false" claims is black women. For a black woman to be a poet is a blessing of continuity as is truth-telling, no matter what the cost or unease at the reclamation and enunciation of crimes. To ritualize these increments, at a level of design, is high artistry. What the people make will carry the collective tune.

"Photographs: A Vision of Massacre": The war in Vietnam was teleported into American consciousness by photojournalism and television coverage, still photography and motion sickness. We need to assess, and be grateful for, images that give clarity, so as not to be imprisoned in false reconstructions of events.

"The Dance of the Elephants": Susan Kirschner told the story of an elephant childhood toy. She was born in Seattle on June 21, 1944, to parents who escaped the Nazis. Her parents were both doctors (also musicians). The story was told to cure her of the nightmare she had about what happened to her parents.

"House on Miramar, San Francisco": The poem is located in the body of the mother: workbench. The outside world represents the back and front views on reality: flowers in the back—dahlias, bulbs—and the mother's nursery, for her children and for her recovery. She is nursing the living and the dead, her connections to her children. The working punctuation of the lines in phrasing assimilates an inner music and hyaline membrane disease (acute respiratory syndrome), which newborn/premature infants suffer. There were two incidents of this—in the second and third sons—in this emerging family.

"Movin' Wes" was written in memory of the guitarist Wes Montgomery and his technical innovations to the jazz guitar.

"Newsletter from My Mother: *8:30 A.M., December 8, '69*" is in quotation marks because it is a verbatim transcript of my mother's iteration of events while she was at work in the Los Angeles County Hospital.

"*'Bird Lives':* Charles Parker in St. Louis": "Bird Lives" was scribbled on walls during the forties as an anthem of freedom from restrictions, including racial bigotry. The scene is St. Louis in the early fifties in a Mafia-controlled nightclub where Parker is expected to enter the establishment through the kitchen, not the front door. After two consecutive incidents in which Bird overturned (by accident) a huge vat of tomato paste on the kitchen floor, he was instructed to use the front—hence a special brand of desegregation was instituted in the Gateway to the West. This poem was part of a cycle entitled "High Modes." The original design of this cycle was intended to update and critique the classical conceit of the nine muses—hence, the nine parts in the original composition. "*'Bird Lives':* Charles Parker in St. Louis" is the entry of this updating; "High Modes: Vision as Ritual: Confirmation" is the exit.

"High Modes: Vision as Ritual: Confirmation": Black American musicians have easy access to modes because they are self-induced environments that thrive on self-expression. A mode is thus an environment that can be entered and exited as one improvises against a thematic base, sometimes called "the head of a tune." In the recording industry one calls these moments airchecks, particularly for live broadcasts on radio. The essence of a mode and the modality of environment is the power extant to transformation. What is most mysterious about jazz is its African elements, seemingly without language, except in music. "Contact-high" is the resonant humanism transfixed and transcended in the energy of musicmaking. The title comes from a composition by the saxophonist Hank Mobley, who played for a time with Miles Davis. This poem was written for the painter and sculptor Oliver Jackson, a classmate of the poet at Iowa, 1961. Mr. Jackson and the poet collaborated on many of the ideas expressed in the African continuum. This poem originally appeared in a poem cycle entitled "High Modes." The nine-part cycle was an attempt to update and critique the classical conceit of the nine muses. "'Bird Lives': Charles Parker in St. Louis" and "High Modes: Vision as Ritual: Confirmation" are the entry and exit of this updating.

Song: I Want a Witness

"Song: *I Want a Witness*": The antecedent of the poem is the 1967 Detroit riots and the testimony of Ralph Dickey, pianist, composer, poet, and translator of Paul Celan, who confessed his fear during several neighborhood outbursts in which he was ashamed at his sins of omission, at not joining in the carnage. A cycle of poems about Dickey's dilemma can be found in "Approximations" (*Nightmare Begins Responsibility*); another vestige of the riots is "The Algiers Motel Incident: Detroit."

"Oak" was suggested by several visits, in summer, from Thomas McGrath with his son, whom he called "Tomacito."

"Homage to the New World": This poem refers to a verbatim incident in 1971 in the faculty housing complex at the University of Illinois at Urbana-Champaign, where the poet was in residence at the Center for Advanced Study.

"Photographs: *Negatives*": This poem cycle takes place in Dighton, Massachusetts. Unbeknownst to the poet, he is living on an ancient burial ground and cranberry bog, in preparation for the birth of his daughter, Rachel, where photo processing is examined against the backdrop of Roger Williams's break from the Massachusetts Bay Colony, an updating of perspective, and an appropriation of the spiritual worldview of the first indigenes, often without complete acknowledgment. The cycle was conceived in nine parts and was influenced by the nine muses.

Debridement

All the poems printed here from *Debridement* form a section entitled "Heartblow," which is a poetic evaluation of the innovations of the novelist Richard Wright. The nine parts are meant to approximate an updating of the nine muses in race relations and race ritual terminology. "Afterword: A Film" serves as a cadenza to the cycle.

Nightmare Begins Responsibility

"Landfill" was written after the poet, with neighbors in a volunteer fire unit, controlled and finally put out a range fire (fire started for weed control), which got out of hand during the summer.

"Abe": This poem was written for Abraham Chapman, the anthologist of *Black Voices* and *New Black Voices*, among others, and his wife, Belle. The Chapmans gave Richard Wright room and board while he wrote *Black Boy*. They were also present at the ninetieth birthday of Du Bois in Peking (now Beijing).

"From a Town in Minnesota": The poem was inspired by the state signs depicting the great Sioux rebellion, particularly Little Crow. For several generations the state guide had no black or "Indian" presence, but rather a hierarchy of ethnic groups with Germans at the top. One visits Native American "reservations" by invitation only, and under separate statutes of behavior, particularly when using weapons.

"Black Cryptogram" was stolen from the poet/raconteur Sterling A. Brown in conversation.

"Blackjack": *Blackjack*—which can't be found in the dictionary—is an imaginative contraction meant to conjure a collective reality, one resonant in the future (the poet's daughter, Robinson's wife/widow) as trusteeship to an abiding developmental democracy, and certainly more than written down on the page of confrontation (1963), a repeat of 1947. There are leaps in the poem equivalent to Robinson's Pacific Coast broad jump record, which stood for twenty-five years. The poet was a student teaching in Pasadena in 1963, but present in 1947 as a Giants fan, as was his father, but secretly rooting for "the Bums." Robinson was a four-letter man and a hero to more than blacks. He was part of a public trust in a most democratic, nuanced conversation. It is the poet's brother's voice—"Did he say Blackie?"—and a reminder of how kin can't be silenced, or shut up, even in the national pastime, as a bystander.

"Nightmare Begins Responsibility": Though the poet is aware of W. B. Yeats's "Responsibilities" and Delmore Schwartz's "In dreams begin responsibilities," this poem is an expression of personal awareness. It is meant to be read as a mutter; that is, very quickly: cf. Yeats's use of "unutterable"; why the poem is muttered.

"Br'er Sterling and the Rocker" is a folk sonnet highlighting Sterling Brown's poetic inspiration and his "nemesis"—his wife, Daisy.

"Paul Laurence Dunbar: 1872–1906": This poem was written for the centenary of Dunbar's birth and read in Dayton, Ohio.

"Corrected Review: THEREISATREEMOREANCIENTTHANEDEN" is a poetic response and correction to the *New York Times Book Review* in defense of Leon Forrest's narrative improvisations against the founders and their documents, the Constitution, the Bill of Rights, and three-fifths representation of black Americans before the Emancipation Proclamation.

"Alice": This poem was written after a visit in Jackson, Mississippi, during which Alice Walker told the saga of visiting Zora Neale Hurston's grave in Fort Pierce, Florida. Walker wished to anoint the spot with a black onyx stone but was prohibited by cost. The revelation is mythic and literal, calling for protection from snakes in a sodden field.

Images of Kin

"Crossing Lake Michigan": This is a barometric reading of the psychic impact of Martin Luther King Jr.'s assassination.

"Tongue-Tied in Black and White": The poem is a response to John Berryman's false appropriation of dialect in the minstrel tradition, a convention of white men in blackface, and the spine of popular entertainment without respect for true minstrelsy, which is the performance of vaudevilleans as a shorthand—and code—for discussing race rituals as race relations. Berryman's work is a false payment for stereotyping. Artistry is the only appropriation. Bill Robinson (Bo Jangles) was the supreme artist.

"Healing Song" is an honorific for the poet Robert Hayden.

"Uplift from a Dark Tower": The title of this cycle comes from Arthur P. Davis's critical book *From the Dark Tower: Afro-American Writers, 1900 to 1960* on tradition, improvisation, and national memory, including the Indians. Davis's title is a reference to Countee Cullen's poem. "Psychophotos of Hampton" refers to a historical photobook about the early Hampton Institute. Depicted in this book are Plains Indians who perished of "swamp fever" while wards of the Bureau of Indian Affairs at $68 a head, which was part of the national policy of the period.

Healing Song for the Inner Ear

"Double Elegy": This celebrates the poetic nexus of Robert Hayden and James Wright.

"News from Fort Ancient": The poem recalls the mysterious sites of the Indian burial mounds. The woman mentioned in the poem as having tuberculosis of the hip is Ralph Ellison's mother. She was buried in Hillcrest Cemetery, the black cemetery in Cincinnati, Ohio.

"The Loon" was written in memory of Ruth McLaughlin.

"Camp Story": This is for the poet's father, W. Warren Harper, and in memory of the poet's brother, Jonathan.

"The Drowning of the Facts of a Life": This poem is also in memory of the poet's brother, Jonathan Paul Harper, 1941–77, who died in a motorcycle accident in Los Angeles.

"Horse-Trading" is in memory of the poet Henri Coulette, the poet's undergraduate teacher. "Horse-trading" was Henri Coulette's moniker for Paul Engle's workshop activities and raising money for the Iowa Writers' Workshop. Coulette wrote devastating formal sequences on the understory of workshop/faculty politics, mostly in the sestina form. "Intaglio" was an influence on the poet by the invention of a new rhyme scheme and framing strategy while describing another artistic medium, the intaglio process.

"Hooking": This is a poetic eulogy for Nellie Shannon, who was one of the mainstays of the Yaddo artist colony.

"Stepto's Veils": The art of criticism is the problem of the twenty-first century (a play on Du Bois's "The problem of the twentieth century is the problem of the color line.") Also, this poem is related to "Uplift from a Dark Tower."

"The Body Polity," "The Pen," and " 'Goin' to the Territory' " are all influenced by the life and times of Ralph Ellison.

"My Book on Trane" cycle: The spirit of this sequence is the consciousness of McCoy Tyner during his time as the main pianist with the John Coltrane quartet, 1961–65.

"Stutterer": These stanzas were written while the poet was under detention in Soweto.

"The Militance of a Photograph in the Passbook of a Bantu under Detention": The poem was suggested by a brief visit to the house John Albert Johnson lived in at Evaton while he was a missionary for the AME Church, 1908–16. Johnson built Fannie Coppin Hall, a girls' residence and the first building at Wilberforce Institute in Evaton. He bought the land under freehold legal provisions before the Union of South Africa became a union. Therefore, this parcel was the only land that belonged to blacks during the apartheid era. The following is a letter written by Johnson during his stay:

> Greetings:
> I have the honor to submit the following for your information and consideration: For the past eleven months the country has suffered a severe drought which has destroyed the harvest; killed cattle, sheep, and game in many districts. The poor facilities for transportation in some sections greatly embarrassed the efforts to forward relief in the form of provision. The lack of water was an aggravating form of suffering.
>   A number of our missionaries could not reach the seat of Conference which met in Bloemfontein, Orange Free State, in the end of November, 1912.

During the past year four of our most efficient elders have died, among them Rev. Henry C. Misikinya, a graduate of Wilberforce University. Two others withdrew under charges, and six were expelled—four natives and two colored—thereby decreasing our ministerial ranks by twelve, a serious loss to our working force.

This lay membership increased several hundred and the financial reports showed an increase over last year.

The attitude of Parliament toward the native and colored residents of the Union is reflected somewhat in the passing of a Bill prohibiting any European from selling or leasing any land to a colored or native person; or any colored or native person selling or leasing to a European; restricting travel; and prohibiting a non-resident in a location from remaining over twenty-four hours.

In several cases recently, municipalities have refused a church site to any religious body which does not have a European at its head. Several of our large congregations have been scattered thereby, notably Pretoria and Heidelburg in Transvaal. Pretoria paid over $300 in Dollar Money at the last Conference.

The care of all the churches under such conditions involves much visitation, and the encouragement of much expenditure.

I am earnestly endeavoring to serve our Lord and Church. I do not hesitate to confess my deep sense of need of your prayers for patience and perseverance, and above all, for the grace of God.

I am, dear brethren,

> Your fellow laborer,
> J. Albert Johnson
> South Africa, March, 1913

"A Narrative of the Life and Times of John Coltrane: Played by Himself," "Driving the Big Chrysler across the Country of My Birth," and "Peace on Earth" are all influenced by the itinerary of John Coltrane's famous quartet—John Coltrane, reeds; Elvin Jones, drums; McCoy Tyner, piano; Jimmy Garrison, bass.

Honorable Amendments

"Intentional Suffering": The golden rule made flesh: prayer, service, nonviolence. The notion of suffering beginning with forgiveness, the Dexter Avenue Church extending invitation to former governor George Wallace to appear before the congregation and ask, and be granted, forgiveness for his white supremacist posturing. Ethical teaching is the answer to a violent culture.

"To an Old Man Twiddlin' Thumbs": This refers to the poet Sterling Brown. The last line echoes Brown's anthem "Strong Men."

"Angola (Louisiana)" was inspired by the fiction of Ernest J. Gaines, a native of Louisiana.

"Portrait of James Weldon Johnson": Johnson's career is suggested by an archival photograph from 1920. Johnson's wife, Grace Nail, gave a rocking chair to the poet's maternal grandmother at the birth of Barrett Johnson, the poet's uncle, born 1911. Johnson's fluency with the conceits of protocol, and cultural exchange, was not documented in his autobiographical writing.

"Archives" ends with a proverbial affirmation assigned to Ernie Banks, the Chicago Cubs Hall of Famer; it is also a code for the attitude of all ballplayers connected with the Negro Leagues—a call for all comers. The poem was written for the poet's son, Patrice Cuchulain Harper, fifteen and a high school baseball and football player in Hamilton, N.Y.

"The Ghost of Soul-Making": This is a trope taken from John Keats's letters—"The Vale of Soulmaking." Ruth Oppenheim is a survivor of Kristallnacht, which she witnessed as a child.

"Studs": The title connotes diamond earrings, but also the nuanced undertones of musicians, on the road, in ensemble units, who had parts to play in "charts" both written and improvised, with extended solos that were not recorded, suggesting that, in the progression of creativity, the best music is unrecorded.

"My Father's Face": Schomburg was best friend of the poet's grandfather, Roland Johnson, whose father, John Albert Johnson, was a founding member of the Black American Academy and an AME bishop. The bishop's papers, books, and sermons were donated to the Schomburg Library by bequest and the poet's father itemized and deposited them. Allusions to Nat King Cole, a native of Montgomery, Alabama, and the monument to slain civil rights workers designed by Maya Lin, architect of the Vietnam Memorial, are deliberate.

"Thimble": The poem refers to Henrietta Bowers, the first black undertaker in the United States, a resident of Philadelphia, and a conductor on the underground railroad. She was the maternal ancestor of the poet's mother.

Peace Gene

"Irish Suit": The poem refers to an actual Irish suit that the poet had made in Dublin. The suit was made of Irish wool and had lined pants for warmth.

"Strands": The poem echoes the poetic and historical conceits of William Butler Yeats as reported by his critics.

"Aborigines (Estonia)": Aborigines as defined by President Meri are not native peoples, but individual writers.

"*marginalia*": The poem was written in Key West, Florida, in the house of Fannie and Ralph Ellison during the Gulf War, 1991. Mr. Ellison's persona is resonant because he shares a birthday with Richard Wilbur.

"An Umbrella of Maple Leaves": Cleophus is one of the transcendent characters in Ralph Ellison's fiction.

"The Writer's Desk": There is a psychic connection between this poem and "An Umbrella of Maple Leaves."

"Paradise (Gihon River, Johnson, Vermont)": This poem was written in memory of Roger Rath, who died in a traffic accident while teaching at Johnson State University, Johnson, Vermont.

"Letter of Athenaeum Couplets in Memory of William Strickland" was written for the architect of the Providence Athenaeum private library.

"Day Room: St. Elizabeths Hospital": Some details in the poem were provided by Jewelnel Davis when she was a novice at St. Elizabeths Hospital. Chaplain Davis presides at Columbia University, New York City.

"Sorbet," "Double Sorbet," "Triple Sorbet," "Wizardry: The Poetic Saga in Song of Gwendolyn Brooks," and "The Poet's Voice" were written as a cycle for Gwendolyn Brooks's birthday.

"Peace Plan: Meditation on the Nine Stages of 'Peacemaking' as a Tribute to Senator *Claiborne Pell:* January 9, 1997": This poem was read at the PELL AWARDS for Excellence in the Arts, January 9, 1997, at the Westin Hotel in Providence and sponsored by Trinity Repertory Company and its benefactors.

"Notes on Making: The Heroic Pattern Updated: 1997" was commissioned by Joseph Norman for *Monologue 2,* the catalog to an art exhibition at Cornell University, 1997.

"Judicial Assignment" was written for the occasion of Ojetta Rogeriee Thompson's initiation as associate justice of the Superior Court in Rhode Island.

"Patrice Lumumba": The poem intends to document the pictorial and psychic demands of a new revolutionary leadership annihilated while in the bud and the forces enlisted in power control.

"Frederick Douglass Cycle": This was commissioned by the historian David Blight of Amherst College to commemorate the one hundredth anniversary of the death of Frederick Douglass.

"Dream: Bicentennial, Rochester, N.Y. (after F.D. Residence Fire)" is a remembrance of Judith Kitchen, reviewer for the *Georgia Review*.

"Figments": This is a eulogy composed on the death of Charles Twichell Davis, master of Calhoun College, Yale University.

If You Don't Force It

"On First Listening to *Native Dancer* by Wayne Shorter" is dedicated to John O. Stewart, novelist, anthropologist, teacher, friend.

"Relaxing with R.B.S. over Tunes": This is a birthday tune to Robert Stepto on his birthday, October 28, 1997, sent by fax, written on the back of an insurance form.

"Homage to Mamie Owens": Mamie Owens is the paternal grandmother of the poet's father.

"10's & Things": A virtuoso musician, Carmen McCrae was intimidated by the artistry of Billie Holiday. She was a distinctive improviser on the keyboard as well.

Index of Titles

Abe 104
Aborigines (Estonia) 229
Achebe at the Bridge 280
Advice to Clinton 288
Afterword: A Film 96
Alice 119
Alone 5
American History 19
Angola (Louisiana) 198
Archives 212
Arpeggios 169
Arrival 338
At the Cemetery 70
At the Moment 346
Audio 327

Bandstand 168
The Battle of Saratoga (Springs)
   Revisited 131
Biafra Blues 29
Bigger's Blues 90
"Bird Lives": Charles Parker in St. Louis 50
The Black Angel 11
Black Cryptogram 108
Blackjack 111
Black Spring 17
Blues Alabama 18
The Body Polity 162
The Borning Room 73
Br'er Sterling and the Rocker 115
Brother John 3

Calligraphy 252
Camp Story 150
Cinco de Mayo 342
Clark's Way West: Another Version 12
A Coltrane Poem: September 23, 1998 365
Corrected Review:
   THEREISATREEMOREANCIENT-
   THANEDEN 117
Crossing Lake Michigan 123

The Dance of the Elephants 42
Day Room: St. Elizabeths Hospital 246
Dead Oaks 59
Dear John, Dear Coltrane 25
Dear Romie: Rock Formation Epistles 208
Deathwatch 22
Dining from a Treed Condition, an Histor-
   ical Survey 132
Discovery 10
Double Elegy 143
Double Sorbet 257
The Douglass Position, 1863 297
Dream: Bicentennial, Rochester, N.Y. (after
   F.D. Residence Fire) 311
Driving the Big Chrysler across the Coun-
   try of My Birth 189
The Drowning of the Facts of a Life 152

Elvin's Blues 7
"Engagements" 173

The Families Album 74
Faulkner's Centennial Poem: September 25,
   1997 282
55: The Journey Motif in My Sister's Birth-
   day Song June 6, 1998 352
Figments 313
For Bud 9
The Founding Fathers in Philadelphia 134
Frederick Douglass Cycle 294
"Frederick, Is God Dead?" 307
From a Town in Minnesota 106

The Ghost of Soul-Making 214
"Goin' to the Territory" 165
Grandfather 109

Healing Song 128
Heartblow 85
Heartblow: Messages 93
Here Where Coltrane Is 37

The Hidden Friends of Frederick Douglass 299
High Modes: Vision as Ritual: Confirmation 52
History as Apple Tree 80
History as Bandages: Polka Dots and Moonbeams 36
History as Diabolical Maternalism 92
Homage to Mamie Owens 344
Homage to the Brown Bomber 202
Homage to the New World 65
Hooking 158
Horse-Trading 157
House on Miramar, San Francisco 44
How to Forgive the Father Who Screams at His Son 360

If You Don't Force It 325
In Hayden's Collage 147
Intentional Suffering 195
Irish Suit 225
I was born in the same house as my mother, and delivered by the same man 340

John Hope Franklin 284
Journey through the Interior 204
Judicial Assignment 286

Kin 101
Kneading 58

Landfill 103
Last Affair: Bessie's Blues Song 63
Letter of Athenaeum Couplets in Memory of William Strickland 244
The Loon 149
The Love Letters of Helen Pitts Douglass 295
Love Medley: Patrice Cuchulain 34
Love Postcard while Listening to "Autumn Leaves" 358

Madimba: Gwendolyn Brooks 39
marginalia 231
Martin's Blues 38
Matchbook: The Spinnaker (Sausalito) 329
The Meaning of Protest 88
Meditation on Auburn Prison (for Harriet Tubman) 304
Messages as Translation 250

The Militance of a Photograph in the Passbook of a Bantu under Detention 184
Molasses and the Three Witches 24
A Mother Speaks: The Algiers Motel Incident, Detroit 27
Movin' Wes 46
Mr. P.C. 28
Mr. P.C., 1942–98, Bard College 278
My Book on Trane (poem) 180
My Book on Trane (poem cycle) 167
My Father's Face 218
My Mother's Bible 335

A Narrative of the Life and Times of John Coltrane: Played by Himself 187
Near the White House 87
The Negatives 67
News from Fort Ancient 145
Newsletter from My Mother: 8:30 A.M., December 8, '69 48
Nightmare Begins Responsibility 114
The Night of Frost 69
Notes on Making: The Heroic Pattern Updated: 1997 273

Oak 61
Obscurity 172
Odd Facts about the Painter (On Causality) 206
On First Listening to Native Dancer by Wayne Shorter 331

Parable 91
Paradise (Gihon River, Johnson, Vermont) 237
Patrice Lumumba 290
Paul Laurence Dunbar: 1872–1906 116
Peace on Earth 191
Peace Plan: Meditation on the Nine Stages of "Peacemaking" as a Tribute to Senator Claiborne Pell: January 9, 1997 270
The Pen 163
Photographs 68
Photographs: A Vision of Massacre 41
Photographs: Negatives 66
Pocahontas (Tuscaloosa, Alabama) 239
The Poet's Voice 263
Polls 170
Portrait of James Weldon Johnson 210
Prayer: Mt. Hood and Environs 33

Preaching at the Funeral (Songs of the
 Choir in Silent Prayer) 301
Prestige 174
Psychophotos of Hampton 136
Pullman Pass 155
Pulp Notes 178

Queries to Alice Elizabeth: An Obituary,
 Palm Sunday, 1998 348
Quilting Bee (Mecklenburg County) 201

Rat Fever: History as Hallucination 86
Reading from Isherwood's Letter Circa
 1959–63 264
Reading Jean Toomer's *Cane* Again 292
Relaxing with R.B.S. over Tunes 333
Release: Kind of Blue 363
Remember Mexico 13
Reuben, Reuben 23
Rhythmic Arrangements (On Prosody) 242
Rose: May 17, 1998 350
Rumors 175

Shaharazad 356
"Sinatra" (1915–98) 269
Sled 241
Solo 171
Song: *I Want a Witness* 57
Songlines from a Tessera(e) Journal:
 Romare Bearden, 1912–88 200
Sorbet 255

Spiritual 95
Stepto's Veils 160
Strands 227
Studs 216
Stutterer 182
Sugarloaf 176

10's & Things 362
Thimble 220
This Is My Son's Song: *"Ungie, Hi
 Ungie"* 35
To an Old Man Twiddlin' Thumbs 197
Tongue-Tied in Black and White 125
Trays: A Portfolio 75
Tree Fever 89
Triple Sorbet 259

An Umbrella of Maple Leaves 233
Uplift from a Dark Tower 130
Utility Room 72

Village Blues 6
Voice 354

We Assume: On the Death of Our Son,
 Reuben Masai Harper 20
Wizardry: The Poetic Saga in Song of
 Gwendolyn Brooks 261
The Writer's Desk 235

Zocalo 15

Illinois Poetry Series
Laurence Lieberman, Editor

History Is Your Own Heartbeat
Michael S. Harper (1971)

The Foreclosure
Richard Emil Braun (1972)

The Scrawny Sonnets and Other Narratives
Robert Bagg (1973)

The Creation Frame
Phyllis Thompson (1973)

To All Appearances: Poems New and Selected
Josephine Miles (1974)

The Black Hawk Songs
Michael Borich (1975)

Nightmare Begins Responsibility
Michael S. Harper (1975)

The Wichita Poems
Michael Van Walleghen (1975)

Images of Kin: New and Selected Poems
Michael S. Harper (1977)

Poems of the Two Worlds
Frederick Morgan (1977)

Cumberland Station
Dave Smith (1977)

Tracking
Virginia R. Terris (1977)

Riversongs
Michael Anania (1978)

On Earth as It Is
Dan Masterson (1978)

Coming to Terms
Josephine Miles (1979)

Death Mother and Other Poems
Frederick Morgan (1979)

Goshawk, Antelope
Dave Smith (1979)

Local Men
James Whitehead (1979)

Searching the Drowned Man
Sydney Lea (1980)

With Akhmatova at the Black Gates
Stephen Berg (1981)

Dream Flights
Dave Smith (1981)

More Trouble with the Obvious
Michael Van Walleghen (1981)

The American Book of the Dead
Jim Barnes (1982)

The Floating Candles
Sydney Lea (1982)

Northbook
Frederick Morgan (1982)

Collected Poems, 1930–83
Josephine Miles (1983; reissue, 1999)

The River Painter
Emily Grosholz (1984)

Healing Song for the Inner Ear
Michael S. Harper (1984)

The Passion of the Right-Angled Man
T. R. Hummer (1984)

Dear John, Dear Coltrane
Michael S. Harper (1985)

Poems from the Sangamon
John Knoepfle (1985)

In It
Stephen Berg (1986)

The Ghosts of Who We Were
Phyllis Thompson (1986)

Moon in a Mason Jar
Robert Wrigley (1986)

Lower-Class Heresy
T. R. Hummer (1987)

Poems: New and Selected
Frederick Morgan (1987)

Furnace Harbor: A Rhapsody of the North
    Country
Philip D. Church (1988)

Bad Girl, with Hawk
Nance Van Winckel (1988)

Blue Tango
Michael Van Walleghen (1989)

Eden
Dennis Schmitz (1989)

Waiting for Poppa at the Smithtown Diner
Peter Serchuk (1990)

Great Blue
Brendan Galvin (1990)

What My Father Believed
Robert Wrigley (1991)

Something Grazes Our Hair
S. J. Marks (1991)

Walking the Blind Dog
G. E. Murray (1992)

The Sawdust War
Jim Barnes (1992)

The God of Indeterminacy
Sandra McPherson (1993)

Off-Season at the Edge of the World
Debora Greger (1994)

Counting the Black Angels
Len Roberts (1994)

Oblivion
Stephen Berg (1995)

To Us, All Flowers Are Roses
Lorna Goodison (1995)

Honorable Amendments
Michael S. Harper (1995)

Points of Departure
Miller Williams (1995)

Dance Script with Electric Ballerina
Alice Fulton (reissue, 1996)

To the Bone: New and Selected Poems
Sydney Lea (1996)

Floating on Solitude
Dave Smith (3–vol. reissue, 1996)

Bruised Paradise
Kevin Stein (1996)

Walt Whitman Bathing
David Wagoner (1996)

Rough Cut
Thomas Swiss (1997)

Paris
Jim Barnes (1997)

The Ways We Touch
Miller Williams (1997)

The Rooster Mask
Henry Hart (1998)

The Trouble-Making Finch
Len Roberts (1998)

Grazing
Ira Sadoff (1998)

Turn Thanks
Lorna Goodison (1999)

Traveling Light: Collected and New Poems
David Wagoner (1999)

Some Jazz a While: Collected Poems
Miller Williams (1999)

The Iron City
John Bensko (2000)

Songlines in Michaeltree: New and Collected
Poems
Michael S. Harper (2000)

Pursuit of a Wound
Sydney Lea (2000)

The Pebble: Old and New Poems
Mairi MacInnes (2000)

National Poetry Series

Eroding Witness
Nathaniel Mackey (1985)
Selected by Michael S. Harper

Palladium
Alice Fulton (1986)
Selected by Mark Strand

Cities in Motion
Sylvia Moss (1987)
Selected by Derek Walcott

The Hand of God and a Few
Bright Flowers
William Olsen (1988)
Selected by David Wagoner

The Great Bird of Love
Paul Zimmer (1989)
Selected by William Stafford

Stubborn
Roland Flint (1990)
Selected by Dave Smith

The Surface
Laura Mullen (1991)
Selected by C. K. Williams

The Dig
Lynn Emanuel (1992)
Selected by Gerald Stern

My Alexandria
Mark Doty (1993)
Selected by Philip Levine

The High Road to Taos
Martin Edmunds (1994)
Selected by Donald Hall

Theater of Animals
Samn Stockwell (1995)
Selected by Louise Glück

The Broken World
Marcus Cafagña (1996)
Selected by Yusef Komunyakaa

Nine Skies
A. V. Christie (1997)
Selected by Sandra McPherson

Lost Wax
Heather Ramsdell (1998)
Selected by James Tate

So Often the Pitcher Goes to Water until It
Breaks
Rigoberto González (1999)
Selected by Ai

Other Poetry Volumes

Local Men and *Domains*
James Whitehead (1987)

Her Soul beneath the Bone: Women's Poetry
on Breast Cancer
Edited by Leatrice Lifshitz (1988)

Days from a Dream Almanac
Dennis Tedlock (1990)

Working Classics: Poems on Industrial Life
Edited by Peter Oresick and Nicholas Coles
(1990)

Hummers, Knucklers, and Slow Curves:
    Contemporary Baseball Poems
Edited by Don Johnson (1991)

The Double Reckoning of Christopher
    Columbus
Barbara Helfgott Hyett (1992)

Selected Poems
Jean Garrigue (1992)

New and Selected Poems, 1962–92
Laurence Lieberman (1993)

The Dig and *Hotel Fiesta*
Lynn Emanuel (1994)

For a Living: The Poetry of Work
Edited by Nicholas Coles and Peter Oresick
(1995)

The Tracks We Leave: Poems on Endangered
    Wildlife of North America
Barbara Helfgott Hyett (1996)

Peasants Wake for Fellini's *Casanova* and
    Other Poems
*Andrea Zanzotto; edited and translated by John
    P. Welle and Ruth Feldman; drawings by
    Federico Fellini and Augusto Murer* (1997)

Moon in a Mason Jar and *What My Father
    Believed*
Robert Wrigley (1997)

The Wild Card: Selected Poems, Early and
    Late
*Karl Shapiro; edited by Stanley Kunitz and
    David Ignatow* (1998)

Turtle, Swan and *Bethlehem in Broad Daylight*
Mark Doty (2000)

Typeset in 10.5/13 Minion
with Minion display
Designed by Paula Newcomb
Composed by Celia Shapland
for the University of Illinois Press
Manufactured by Thomson-Shore, Inc.

University of Illinois Press
1325 South Oak Street
Champaign, IL 61820-6903
www.press.uillinois.edu